IN RINGWALT'S GORGEOUSLY AMBITIOUS BOOK, *The Wheel*, awakening is not a thing to be attained; it is a perpetual unfolding—both backwards and forwards—through time. These pages do not so much contain language but rather a dream of language, conveying something without actually being able to say it. It is a work of divination in the truest sense, a speech 'to fill this space with bells, with olive trees.' And just as we disappear within its descent, we find grace.

JANAKA STUCKY, AUTHOR OF *ASCEND ASCEND* AND PUBLISHER OF BLACK OCEAN

AM RINGWALT'S WORDS GIVE US TALISMANS for so many occasions, turns of phrase, verbal images to tuck away for later, for now, for the past as it returns again. In reading *The Wheel* you become caught in its rhythms as it delves into the whirlpool of stories we each contain and must, at some point, reckon with. Ringwalt invokes a number of artists and writers in her journey but none more than Dante himself, giving us a touch of religion with the magic, and playing Virgil herself as she carries us through a reflection of the un-doing and rebuilding that our lives so often are.

ALLISON GRIMALDI DONAHUE, TRANSLATOR OF CARLA LONZI'S *SELF-PORTRAIT*

CIRCLING THROUGH MEMORY, TRAUMA, LOVE AND CREATION, AM Ringwalt's *The Wheel* leads with an I that is 'ambivalent and vigilant at once'—one whose capacity to embody rigor and uncertainty compels a dynamic between author and reader akin to the two-way transmission of a live performance. *Are you with me?* she asks, slicing through the poly-vocal weave of first-person narrative, poems, emails, photographs and embedded quotations. Such moments of direct address in *The Wheel* are both bracing and generous, letting readers decide whether to re-enforce or transcend their own imagined borders. In this vibrant, collaborative book, Ringwalt rejects repressive frameworks and fixed categories in favor of flux states, and the possibilities of breaking through, of connection. I keep returning to *The Wheel*, exhilarated by the pleasure of 'attending to a turning thing… a moving thing' with Ringwalt, and by the shocks of discovery that accompany each reading.

BRIDGET TALONE, AUTHOR OF *A SOFT LIFE*

AM RINGWALT'S THE WHEEL is a gentle invitation to listen, to listen to life as a song, as a constellation of songs. Reaching out in time and space, *The Wheel* gracefully embraces us with the touch of the human and the divine, guiding us to cross familiar states of presence and move towards the discovery of deeper possible ones.

POUPEH MISSAGHI, AUTHOR OF *TRANS(RE)LATING HOUSE ONE*

The Wheel

AM Ringwalt

Spuyten Duyvil
New York City

An excerpt of this manuscript first appeared in *Entropy*.

"Notes from the Eclipse" first appeared in *OCCULUM*.

"Via Negativa" first appeared in *Cloud Rodeo*.

Like Cleopatra was published by dancing girl press.

The Wheel was longlisted for Tarpaulin Sky's 2020 Book Awards.

© 2021 AM Ringwalt
ISBN 978-1-952419-53-9

cover art © Niki Current

Library of Congress Cataloging-in-Publication Data

Names: Ringwalt, Anne Malin, author.
Title: The wheel / A.M. Ringwalt.
Description: New York City : Spuyten Duyvil, [2021] | Autobiographical creative nonfiction essays. |
Identifiers: LCCN 2020054815 | ISBN 9781952419539 (paperback)
Subjects: LCSH: Ringwalt, Anne Malin.
Classification: LCC CT275.R6067 A3 2021 | DDC 920--dc23
LC record available at https://lccn.loc.gov/2020054815

> We were climbing through a fissure in the stone
> that kept turning from one side to the other
> as a wave that flows out and runs in again.
> *Purgatorio*, Canto X, 7 (trans. Merwin)

> We should help them to wash away the stains
> they took there, so they can be light and pure
> to go out to the wheeling of the stars.
> *Purgatorio*, Canto XI, 34 (trans. Merwin)

> If you don't mind being patient
> with my fumbling around,
> I'll come up singing for you
> > Nina Simone, "Stars" (written by Janis Ian)

We sat on the floor of a spare bedroom in my grandparents' house. The walls were yellow, the bedsheets and curtains decorated with a matching rose-patterned fabric. I could hear the sound of the dryer through the wall, its suggestion of warmth and cleanliness. From a glass cabinet, alongside countless other items, a ceramic figurine of a German Shephard looked toward me. The ceramic dog, a banal emblem of my father's childhood, was the tallest figurine on the shelf. It loomed, simultaneously ambivalent and innocent. I thought about my grandmother in the seventies, walking her German Shephard to the Pacific Ocean, trying to forget. I thought about the olive trees.

Saoli wanted to do a tarot spread. She wanted to light a candle. We didn't have a real one, so I pulled up a video on YouTube: *[10 Hours] Burning Candle – Video Only*. Her deck was decorated with figures from Botticelli paintings. We had been at the beach all day, talking about communication and divination, watching children dash in and out of the ocean. My cheeks were red from the winter sun. Saoli told me about dancing at a club in Los Angeles a few weeks earlier, how a mystic approached her, saying her ancestors were trying to reach her to deliver a message. When she finally met with the mystic, she realized it was bullshit.

My grandmother called me when we were on the beach.
She forgot where I was, when I'd be home.

It's the setting that matters, here, setting-as-catalyst: me on the floor with an old friend in my father's childhood bedroom in Corona del Mar, California, trying to make sense of our lives, Saoli's chipped gold glitter nail polish matching the gold on the Botticelli tarot cards, her right hand reaching for a card to draw. Synthetic candle-flicker. Upside-down-wheel.

The upside-down-wheel propels me through time.

*

I went to Italy, the birth-country of tarot, in the new year. After learning that tarot originated in Milan, and in conjunction with the Italian Renaissance, I wanted to explore resonances between and beyond Christian and Pagan systems of meaning-making. My graduate school provided me with airfare and a small apartment in Rome—a point of convergence between my Italian interests—near Termini Station on via Principe Amedeo. I'd stay for seventeen days. I wondered: what role did tarot and astrology have in meaning-making? What meaning might I find?

After all, the astrological permeated the social fabric of my twenties. On my first day of a World Music seminar as an undergraduate, a boy sitting next to me asked me what my star sign was. Another friend once told me that I was the first Aries they'd met who they liked. Most of my close friends from college, including Saoli, actively read their horoscopes, and sought some kind of beyond-human resonance to accompany and enrich their lives. Saoli studied film, and we made a handful of music videos together when we lived in Boston. Saoli shot the music video for my song "Please" in a church. The video opens with sunlight through stained-glass. Static.

As a sophomore in college, I fixated on Christian symbolism. I dressed up as 'The Virgin Scary' for Halloween: a zombie version of Jesus' mother wearing DIY face paint, a black lace bodysuit and a blue bedsheet as a veil. My friends gave me holographic Jesus prints from Chinatown for my birthday. Despite my kitschy and near-insincere engagement, I identified as religious. The ways in which Christian symbols were commodified in American culture provided ironic materiality to my practice. What mega-Christian corporation benefited from my buying a $5 picture of Mary in Chinatown in Boston? Who was oppressed in the process—of production, of distribution? Still, I collected her: holograms, carvings, coins.

On the other hand, I was drawn to the trance-inducing songs of Taize and the near-sublime Song of Solomon. These repetitions and utterances—*I am dark, but lovely / O daughters of Jerusalem*—helped me understand my femininity, my being. I found transcendence in repetition, trance in alliteration:

My beloved is to me a sachet of myrrh
that lies between my breasts.
My beloved is to me a cluster of henna blossoms
in the vineyards of Engedi.

A church in downtown Boston sometimes commissioned original music and poetry from me, which I was lucky enough to perform as a part of its small but devoted community. I found this church the weekend after the Boston Marathon Bombing when the space opened to the public for a vigil. After a glass of champagne at lunch and struggling to adjust my eyes from the bright sun of Newbury Street to the cave-like interior of the sanctuary, all I heard was a cello. Someone from the New England Conservatory was performing alongside the church's pianist—from Olivier Messiaen's "Quartet for the End of Time."

If I believe in anything, it's the sound of that cello in that space, its reverberations affecting bodies other than my own—and, still, with me. I need you to listen with me.

[*Messiaen: Quartet for the End of Time.* Olivier Messiaen, Tashi. "Louange à l'immortalité de Jésus"; eight minutes, eleven seconds.]

*

When I arrived in Rome, I got out of a taxi near midnight to meet my friend Kelly outside of my apartment. Even though the sun had set, Rome was bright. Fluorescent lights and flames lit the street. As the days passed, at any given point, I could hear at least one set of church bells resounding through my neighborhood. One morning, at least six sets of bells were resounding. It didn't sound like competition. This kind of saturation, overlapping, interacting, filled me. From my bedroom, often waking, I had no way of knowing where these bells came from. I could trace the streets later, to be sure, wondering which sites were proximal to my bed, but I'd never be certain with dozens of churches nearby. Whatever I believed in, in such moments of saturation, all I could do was sit on my bed and listen—feel the aural tension press through to my bones.

We found a bar a few doors down from my apartment and shared a bottle of wine. Kelly, who I met when we were students at a boarding school in the woods of northern Michigan, was now a doctoral student working in a biology lab. Newly reunited, we reminisced on a modern dance class we took as high schoolers, one where we explored floor-based improvisations and clumsily rolled across linoleum. Our time at boarding school contained some of the worst moments of my life. Still, we clung to our deliberately absurd dance moves, often imitating the motions of deep-sea kelp, which we shamelessly performed around our campus. Strangeness was our protest—to violence, stress, adolescence.

I invited Kelly to join me in Rome over tequila shots in a dive bar in South Bend, Indiana. That night, I performed alongside my then-ex at a performance-venue-cum-warehouse, and Kelly and I snuck away before selling CDs or talking to mutual friends. Kelly, Will and I all went to high school together, and we'd all sleep in my house that night—Kelly with me in my bed, and Will on the couch. Will and I had been performing together for nearly seven years, but this new capacity—of grieving our estrangement from each other while singing songs we wrote in love—gutted me. I sang our "Song of the Siren" to Will's synthesizer rather than my autoharp; its droning affect wound through my veins. I sang, slowly, eyes closed and body swaying: *plunge me into the darkest sea, let me bathe in night. I'll spread my arms like shields of skin and swim my way to light.*

That night, the neon of the dive bar offered respite. It didn't take much convincing to get Kelly onboard for Rome; the moment I asked, she said yes. She knew I'd be reading and writing during our travels, but we didn't talk a lot about my project beforehand. So, on our first night in Italy, I explained my work. Tarot transformed from a court game to an esoteric device in the midst of the Italian Renaissance as once-unquestioning Christians grew critical of the powers of the church. Tarot wasn't always meant for meaning making. I found, in tarot, the capability for earthly symbols and banal materials like playing cards to be re-appropriated for divination. Divination, it seemed, was the profane twin of Catholicism.

At the time, I was thinking of exploring the cultural history and symbology of tarot in conjunction with Dante's *Purgatorio* and Alice Notley's *The Descent of Alette*. As I began my research, though, I realized I needed a textual outlet at once far-reaching and associative. I thought about filling space with symbols—how tarot, Dante and Notley all achieved this, and how I might. Sites that Kelly and I explored in Rome would prove just as instrumental to my symbol-culling as the aforementioned texts: the Capuchin Crypt, the Capitoline Museums, Santa Maria in Trastevere.

We stayed up until four in the morning that first night in Rome, jet-lagged and delighted by our togetherness. When I woke the next day, the sun was bright, church bells resonating both outside the apartment's windows and into my small bedroom. I felt the bells pressing through the glass, easing me awake and outside, where I'd meet Kelly for much-needed sustenance.

*

I only want to fill this space with bells, with olive trees.

*

A few nights into our travels, I remembered that my friend Dario lived in Rome. We met at an arts residency in the Hamptons two summers prior, and I was excited to introduce him to Kelly. When we met up, he grinned and hugged me like I was someone he spoke to daily. In truth, we hadn't spoken in over a year. Still, we felt a closeness—one I hoped to share with Kelly, the three of us bounding out into the night. Immediately, he asked us if we wanted to see his recording studio. We agreed, and following his quick pace, walked a few blocks to a quiet street. His studio was downstairs, and two of his friends were wrapping up a session. Dario quickly led us around, not saying much about the space but proud nonetheless, and soon we were upstairs again, wandering and winding through the neighborhood for drinks and food.

At the bar, I told Dario I had a new song I wanted to share with him. He agreed that we should record it before I left for America. There was an air of excitement to every conversation we had that night; I can't remember the flow in its entirety, but Kelly shared the details of her lab work (rendering spinal cords translucent to isolate and track proteins), and I talked about how much I loved teaching my undergraduates poetry, how shocked they were by our first day's discussion of Ariana Reines' "BARAKA," its "I CAN'T WAIT FOR A MODEST APARTMENT UNDER THE HOLE IN THE ROOF OF THE PANTHEON / A GOLD CHAIN A WISHBONE I CAN'T WAIT FOR MY BIGGEST SCAR TO OPEN ITS BLEEDING MOUTH."

The following day, I sent Dario my song to prepare for our recording session. He said, simply: "I melted." And that kind of melted-ness, that fertile multiplicity, is what I loved about Rome. In my iPhone recording, from somewhere in or out of the apartment I was staying in, a faint droning sound entered into my song. Maybe it was the laundry. Maybe it was electricity. Still, its presence reminded me of the imposition of external sounds—not an aggressive imposition, but a gentle gesture. To move with.

*

Sometimes I hear a song over and over in my sleep. The conscious part of my brain knows what song it is; my subconscious brings it to me in a wave. I wake up hearing it loop in my mind. One post-Rome night, as the snow fell on the ground, I felt stuck. I recalled something a friend told me when I asked her how she was doing: "floating, clogged."

So, I pretended to sleep. I brought a sound into my mind and looped it like a stream. Only through the song's repetition could I rest. It was the way she sings *woman*. It was the birth the song promises: *see my death become a trail, and the trail becomes a flower.* It was the flight. It was the both-ness: *every dreamed and waking hour.*

I'd been back in America for a week, and I felt the spatial shift like an ecstasy-comedown. And it was a manifold force: the fact that, before flying back to the States, I didn't sleep for two days; the fact that I had the flu after fighting a fever on my flight home; the fact that I'd never been in a place I loved as much as Rome, and that I was returning to a place of cold.

I want to say more about all of that, and will.

For now, I want to voice the word *vigil*, defined as "a period of keeping awake during the time usually spent asleep, especially to keep watch or pray."

Staying awake for two whole days—what was I keeping watch over?

> Resonating from the past, a week or years ago:
> The stars vs creatures – Colleen
> Green Rocky Road – Karen Dalton
> Words I Heard – Julia Holter
> terminal paradise – Adrianne Lenker
> from – Adrianne Lenker
> Lemon – Cross Record

*

I applied for a grant to research in Rome—what I called tarot as psychic configuring—when I was stuck. It was August, it was humid and insufferable, and Will was pushing me into a corner I never wanted to be pushed into. I couldn't promise him I'd move somewhere south with him, stay for ten years. We were desperate to save something voiding, void. And he resented me. It was in his eyes, in our lack of touch. It was in the cold, cold way he spoke. He had a parasite, he abjected it, it crawled toward me—both fluid and bodied. I imagined the worst sadness prying my ear open, pouring itself in.

So, I started walking. There aren't many places to walk in South Bend, Indiana. I had three routes that Indiana summer, each a few miles long, and I'd follow at least one each day. I listened to the same music each walk. I walked for the feeling of sweat down my forearms, barely perceptible. I walked for the extreme flushed color my face would take, one that took what felt like hours to subside. These walks became a multiplicitous act of repetition: the same routes, the same songs, and then the sheer fact that walking itself is an act of repetition. One set of movements repeated until the body either can't keep going or decides to rest.

On one particularly humid August walk, I realized I needed an escape route. Something for myself. I considered Rome.

*

The summer I met Dario, two summers ago, I hardly slept. We were at an international arts residency in Southampton, New York with forty or so other artists. We gathered to support the work of Robert Wilson, a theater director known for his militant minimalism. This aesthetic permeated every inch of his Watermill Center, where we worked each day from at least eight in the morning until ten at night. Robert Wilson had a background in architecture, and he considered the landscape surrounding the center something to be meticulously shaped and re-shaped. Landscape, in this pseudo-utopian place, did not connote the natural.

There were rules, which we took great pains to uphold: all trees had to be branch-less until a certain point, the blueberry bushes had to be planted in choreographic order, no dead leaves could be in the gravel, the stones had to be washed. We were preparing the space for the center's annual gala, where artists like Laurie Anderson and Jim Jarmusch and Isabella Rossellini appeared—and performed—in support of Robert Wilson. The social elite of the Hamptons would come in droves, in floor-length silk gowns, for endless champagne, art auctioning, and performances—which we, the participants, gave.

I performed in a dance piece at this event. Two phenomenal dancers—from Greece and France, respectively—had an intricately-arranged, tightly-spaced duet, and a group of ten or so chorus members walked in Robert-Wilson-style as part of the landscape of their movement. Our choreography was painfully slow, monkish, angular. After forty minutes of walking in various hard-wrought lines, my left arm fell completely asleep. Tension, held in the body, has a limit.

Whatever limit I experienced in that dance was soon surpassed by a two-hour-long musical performance I gave on a twelve-foot-tall ladder in the middle of the trees. I had tendinitis from gardening so much and was, until then, terribly afraid of heights. The ladder was dug into the ground, and I was weighed down onto it by a matching fifteen-foot-long silver sequin sheath of fabric, wrapped and pinned around me like a gargantuan gown. The fabric matched my silver guitar, which became—in this weird, alchemical site—both costume and instrument, material and body.

This experience of performing stays in my memory as a kind of ascetic meditation. What I remember, with reverence, is the way my field of vision only contained trees—at the height where leaves could spurt, branches reach. What I remember, with reverence—everything green.

*

Sleep is one of my favorite things to do. Sleep is a vital act of processing the mundane, the traumatic, the inarticulable. So, when I'm in ecstatic sleeplessness, I know I have to pay attention to my environment.

(Voice it again: *setting-as-catalyst*.)

I began thinking about the act of the vigil at Watermill, prompted by the death of poet C. D. Wright. Brian Teare had recently published a reflection on her poetics:

> In 2005, C. D. Wright published her first volume of lyric essays on poetry, *Cooling Time: An American Poetry Vigil*. It's notable, the word *vigil* in its subtitle. The shared root of *vigilant* and *vigilante*, *vigil* in Latin means *awake*, though its subsequent mutations denote everything from night-watchman to insomniac, and its oldest usages in English name the Christian ritual of staying awake the night before a holy day or festival.

I was on Flying Point Beach when I told my friends about this potential for holiness. We had the day off after the gala and were hungover on the sand.

What impressed upon me from these short but overflowing six weeks was the community. We worked ourselves to delirium, community our only relief and—leading up to the performances—parties in a toolshed with rapturous drunkenness, with pink smoke machines, with sex, with sweat, with marijuana. At Flying Point, we could be still. For one, our bodies needed it. I don't remember many of the conversations I had that day, and I think that's the point. I took pictures of my friends in the sun, the blue sky overhead. Cinthya, Deborah, Jokūbas, Barbara.

Cinthya, my closest friend there, sat next to me. Leading up to the gala, we found relief in our landscaping duties by talking about embodiment. We imagined points of convergence between choreography and poetry, performativity and language. Now, the sun clear on our faces, we didn't have to talk about anything.

In his reflection on poem-as-vigil, Teare quotes Wright's poem "Like Hearing Your Name Called in a Language You Don't Understand":

> Comrades, be not in mourning for your being
> to express happiness and expel scorpions is the best job
> on earth.

He talks about the baroque, the biblical, the communal. He writes, and I begin at the 'also':

> And they are also exercises in voice, in compressing the syntax so that disparate levels of diction meld into song. [...] In a move familiar to those who love her voice, the final three lines recall Biblical syntax as well as political speech, harnessing echoes of public rhetoric to affirm the weird work of our being here together.

I love this: "exercises in voice"—the plurality of it, the way in which "voice" necessitates aural movement, articulation. I love that Wright reaches out in affirmation. There's a purifying quality to vigilance; all is attended to, all expression and expulsion alike.

And there's a certain strangeness to the title of Wright's poem: *like hearing your name called in a language you don't understand.* The verb "hearing" suggests a level of the subject's cognition, despite the language barrier. The pronoun "your" indicates a recognition of being named, that one is being called for. Perhaps the title of the poem explicates the very act of vigilance: apprehending something untranslatable while still being affected by its sound, its being. Perhaps vigilance yields feeling rather than knowing.

*

At the park in Trastevere for lunch, Dario told me about a production of Oedipus he just worked on. The performance took place in Naples. I was asking about the trees. I'd seen them in Rome, I'd seen them on my walk from my apartment to Trastevere days before. I'd never seen anything like them before. He said they were pine trees. Stone pines.

"But they're not triangular!" I'd exclaimed, half-joking, dumbfounded.

Seeing these pines—you'd think a whole classification of trees had just mutated in my memory.

Dario told me that various trees behind the amphitheater in Naples were assigned numbers, to be lit as part of the set for Oedipus. Each tree was numbered, colored. A red Tree #3. A blue Tree #4.

*

On stone pines:

My grandfather has dementia. When he was lucid, he made incredible salads. He was a retired lawyer and spent most of his time reading, listening to opera or gardening. He went on walks through the neighborhood, the route my grandmother did with their German shepherd decades earlier.

His advice—never meant as advice—stayed in my memory. Once, as he made a salad, he looked at me and said: "you can never have too many pine nuts."

Another time, once his memory was going, I asked him if there was anything he recently did that he'd like to do again. "Breathe," he said.

*

The trees, numbered. The pine nuts, limitless. Another piece of advice my grandfather gave me: "live life to the full." He didn't have the cliché right—the 'fullest'. I loved the mistranslation.

*

I sang "Wild Mountain Thyme" at Watermill. Giovanni, a theater director from Tuscany, asked if I wanted to spend a few weeks thinking about dreams together. Each day, we gave each other homework—invocations, I called them—to influence each other's dreams. He sent me the music video to Nick Cave and Kylie Minogue's "Where the Wild Roses Grow." I sent him the tarot scene from Alejandro Jodorowsky's "The Holy Mountain."

One afternoon, as we sat in the Watermill Center's meditation garden, I told him I had recently finished a type of psychotherapy that mimicked R.E.M. sleep. By submitting to this kind of hypnosis, my eyes darting from right to left, I could access previously unprocessed memories. At Watermill, I took notes from Robert Wilson's copy of *Thee Psychick BIBLE*, page 212, an encyclopedic entry on sleep:

> One technique we were taught by a Cheyenne/Apache mentor to consciously move into the borderline awake/sleep/dream zone is to lie on your back with your head on a pillow. With your arms in a surrender position, i.e. palms facing up, tips of fingers level with the top of your head, hook the hands under the pillow so they are trapped by your weight. We have found conscious entrance into lucid dreaming states is increased dramatically.

As the culmination of our invocations and conversations, we organized a sleep session for lucid dreaming. Giovanni led a guided meditation. We had been studying Luigi Serafini's *Codex Seraphinianus* for the past few days, and *Codex*-like symbols entered into the meditation: a golden egg, a lack of sky. My singing would wake everyone up—on this fortress of white pillows in a room surrounded by windows. Out the windows, trees.

We all stayed at different houses around the Hamptons, big homes housing ten people each. The social elite of the Hamptons donated their living spaces to Robert Wilson while they went on exotic summer vacations, and we—the broke, hungry artists—lived like characters in a reality TV show. We had swimming pools, hot tubs, balconies. So, to gather at sunrise for a sleep session, Giovanni picked up our volunteers from their respective homes—the few who'd sacrifice what little precious sleep we were able to grasp.

I waited for Giovanni in a state of vigilance, standing on the side of the road at five in the morning. I wanted to watch the sunrise before he picked me up. I leaned against a tree, watched the sky turn from black to grey-green to something brighter. He was running late, so I stood outside for over an hour, listening to the sounds of cars going by.

What made the singing so beautiful? It had little to do with my voice. It had to do with interaction. In the next room—as I found out shortly, near-tears—our friend Dickie was sitting on the floor, his back to the wall, eyes closed. I didn't know he was there. Of course, he knew Marianne Faithfull. Her version of the song cut through me. Nearly a foot shorter than me, and by far the oldest friend I'd ever made, Dickie talked like he was in his twenties while carrying decades of experiences. He always had his saxophone ready for improvisation, collaboration.

When I met Dickie, he asked me where I'd performed my music. I mentioned the Bell House in Brooklyn, where I'd performed at the New Yorker Festival. I mentioned Muchmore's in Williamsburg and the Middle East in Cambridge. When I returned the question, I was mortified; he'd performed with Laurie Anderson, Bob Dylan. He was an original member of the Philip Glass Ensemble. One morning, after seeing Dickie's photography of New York in the 1960s, complete with photos of Philip Glass and Bruce Nauman, I approached Dickie and showed him a tattoo on my forearm. The tattoo was from Nauman's DOE FAWN / FOE DAWN lithograph, and the moment he saw my tattoo, he patted it. With his Louisiana accent he mused: "far out."

As I sang "Wild Mountain Thyme," a disembodied sound came drifting through the room. Dickie was harmonizing with me. Here I was, hearing a sound I didn't anticipate—hearing a sound, wondering if it was part of my voice, if something was aurally transforming. Realizing it was out-of-body, uncontrollable, fluid.

*

After Watermill, I listened obsessively to Colleen's *A flame my love, a frequency*. One of its songs begins: "the stars will have the last word." I had no idea what astrology would mean to me at the time, no idea that tarot would resonate with me or pull me back through the past, or into the present, or wheeling toward the future. When Will picked me up at the end of my residency to move to South Bend, I was overwhelmed as I held echoes of my community fragmenting around the world. Our cross-country move coincided with a solar eclipse. I wrote a poem about it: 'Notes from the Eclipse'. The stars would follow suit, another movement of the wheel.

Is it fog or sea spray
                spreading
                over sand?
The pink moon
                or the green trees?

His eyes, across the fire,
                dark, darting
                to me.
Remember: a lightning-struck tree
on fire.

What you did dream? His English, bent—
I did dream. What I did:

                a white moth,
                glowing

                in my hair,
                neck just kissed.

Remember: the tree at Watermill among others much taller. Its spiraling trunk.

Lips like wind, imperceptible. Remember:
                              how do you feel
a year? I drew a circle
                    with smaller circles in it. The biggest:
the overarching feeling. Its smaller
                              compartments: those and
that which moved me to different degrees
                                        within the over-
arching.

Before the eclipse, I find myself sitting on another tree, face to the sun
as it sets. An hour passes. Another. Watch two white moths circle
each other. Hovering spiral / halo

                        the brooding dove
stretched over sea
                 San Juan / marijuana in thunderstorm
                                              / candied guava
                    / agave pooled
                            Pentecost
                                   dove out-
                                       stretched above
              Atlantic olive branches
                              charred lemongrass
                                        cathedral in a car

                         Faster—

A young girl in white, surrounded by men, dancing bomba.

Remember, please, my body on pillows.

And the party goes on. Spin: like a beam of light evaporating into dusk.

Some rural road in Pennsylvania: I smoke in the passenger seat, windows rolled down, red glitter sunglasses on. The wind carries my hair, lifts open my skull—fluid as dust, as algae in the Montauk tide. Ask: what is more human than loss? What, humane?

My skull: water, dust, moss, dusk?

Overcome in the garden, I inhale, exhale,
                            shrug. *Spallucce*
                            he says, fingers
like moths on my shoulders.
                    (Is it like dusk or like dawn?
                    Through Flying Point
                    or Missoula?)

        I overflow. Drink
                ginseng and mint, cheeks flushed from steam. Gin,
                sing, give me the wind. Give—
                this present my past.

Is it descending light, sea salt, bourbon-bloom, ice-melt?

Is it—

        stay awake long enough for a telephone call
        from light, the lighthouse, *tout ce qui brille*—

        poetry. *Give us back the situations of our dreams*[*]

I dance: slow-

moving as molasses
charged by static, sunset

/ cry to projections of Lou Reed's
voice into green / sway
under stars, hypnotized—O

Molasses, I dance until sunrise, loose-limbed,
eat blood-purple carrots at the beach.

Ice cubes in my palms, O, give—

                    these woods, they know your name, your—
                    (in a dream, say *Here: this is where I kiss you*)

    run
into the ocean
dressed in black lace
        red glitter
        sea foam

                  walk back to shore
                  sand a sanctuary I
                  pray to carry

                  these tongues,
                  dreams (and scream
                  to trees at night,

                  still screaming a silk-
                  strung exhalation)

                  Be Tender[†]—

          wearing these voices always
          around my waist going down
          into sand
                spreading sea foam
                / hands outstretched

/ flowers:
blurring, faster.

I watch an elderly man tease the tide
by approaching the sea, darting away
when too-big waves roll forward. Crash
around his knees. How humble his legs,
his balance.

Fast—

Tender, the party goes on.

I've been dreaming (*remember*).
                                    He drives us to a party in the woods of Long Island,
down an hours-long and spiraled road. To the swimming
                                            pool full of plastic flowers. The
green couch on the green
                grass. *It's better like this*, he says, not kissing.

Driving. Faster. Feels like swimming, or flying,
                                  the windows rolled down.
What I did / who I love
                I fly, swim, cradle, contain.
Moths trace circles on my skull, his finger-flight—
                                      faster. Memory
                    (Is it molasses or silk in the wind?)
abducted into another realm. [‡]

the brooding dove

stretched over

South Bend / Super 8

/ cinnamon roll

/ gasoline this

Good

dove out-

stretched / Friday

crying who?

wine unopened

entering: Fog Area

Is it Green Mountain Road

or Wild Mountain Thyme?

Is it—*I know a man in Galilee*

/ I know a saxophone

humming through the lonesome valley.

Tell me who you love.

South Bend—I sing like it's my church

past Fawn River, Yellow River, Barbie and Napoleon roads. Listen to Rodrigo Amarante's "The Ribbon," crickets outside. Traffic of fog. Ask: what is more unbending than loss? What—unyielding?

Is it dusk or dawn? The party—

                Arezzo,
                Tuscany—

                                If I had
                                a ribbon bow
                                afloat on ship-
                                less oceans / To hide
                                my hair / Did all
                                my best to smile
                                if I had a fancy
                                sash / 'Til your singing
                                eyes and fingers / Drew me
                                loving to your isle[§]

He would find me fair,

            sing *red glitter / sail*
            to me / sail to me—

enfold. Would wish that

                    I sing, flooded red, mountain-wound of being, *here I am*

                    (here I am)

Did I dream he dreamed of me?

                                                                                                            And fair with smile? Now
                                                                                                            my foolish dove

is leaning

                my red glitter dancing

                        / black lace

                        / sea foam

                                                                                   / Touch me not, touch me not,

O my heart, tender I'd lark—

It was raining when Will picked me up in Southampton. He met my friend Deborah at our spectacularly large house, and she told me he seemed like a good man. When I hugged Will, though, I realized I had forgotten the hold of his body. Delirious in the humidity, I dashed upstairs to grab my suitcase and my silver Gretsch guitar—an anniversary gift from Will. The air-conditioning shocked my skin. Whether inside or out, foreignness permeated the air—from the sight of Will in a landscape I'd made a home for myself in, alone, to the knowledge that we had a road-trip ahead of ourselves and an insurmountable amount of tension to live with. I knew Deborah was right, yet I also knew neither of us were happy.

After a day's long traffic driving from Southampton to New Jersey, Will and I camped out at a Super 8. I spent most of the evening crying in bed, unsure of how to process my recent transformations. When I closed my eyes, all I saw were blurs of trees connecting me back to Southampton. Admittedly, Will and I hadn't been happy for months. I wrote poems about not knowing what language to speak to reach him. I felt like a burden.

At Watermill, though, I felt free—like swimming, or flying. I didn't know how to translate that feeling to my commitment to Will; it seemed impossible when he failed to be honest with himself, let alone me, about what he wanted. He didn't even want to move to South Bend.

Still, we had humor. As I wept in the motel bed, Will went to the bathroom and began shaving his beard. He'd poke his head out from the doorway every now and then, modeling nearly a dozen facial hair styles to provoke laughter. I was bewildered that night, recognizing the generosity of Will's behavior while holding an inconsolable ache. I sighed so much that fall, alone and with Will, not sure what I was trying to expel from my lungs, what felt so pressing and un-nameable, in a language I didn't understand.

*

I only want to fill this space with bells, with olive trees, with stone pines, with white pillows.

*

What compels me most about Dante's *Purgatorio* is its movement. Its movement-as-symbol. I see this in the wheel, in the mountain, in the moment when the wheel becomes a verb, and we go out to the wheeling of the stars. If, as from the site of purgatory, Dante looks up, both the wheel—the act of wheeling—and that of the celestial take on religious properties. Practically speaking, the wheeling of the stars may be divine order. The wheeling of the stars may be that which suggests our mortal limits.

Tarot cards, too, spread in constellation-like form. It is from the relation of the cards, their constellating form, where meaning is divined. I want to make sense of myself from sites offered by *Purgatorio* and by tarot alike. I see Alice Notley's T*he Descent of Alette* as one textual intersection of *The Divine Comedy* and tarot, the symbolism and activity of its own card game. Notley's own experience with remembering—her late brother's post-traumatic stress disorder—suggests a link between symbolism and memory, and how a life of active divining (through religious, pagan or harder-to-define modes) moves from circularity to clarity.

My spatial crossing—Corona del Mar, California and Rome, Italy—yields movements backward and forward, a turning through temporalities and their resonances. I gather symbols from this crossing.

*

I only want to fill this space with two white moths, my body on pillows.

*

    The spring after Watermill, Will and I performed in New Orleans and Fayetteville and Little Rock and Tulsa, driving places we'd never been together. One of our shows cancelled last minute, so we went to a record store in Fayetteville and bought a Marianne Faithfull CD: *Before the Poison*. We drove up and around a mountain—White Rock Mountain—to camp for the night. It took over an hour just to drive to the top. The roads were gravel, narrow. The slopes were precarious. I begged him to slow down, over-cautious. We read each other's tarot cards, clumsy, at a picnic table on the top. I don't remember what we wanted to find out. We walked around the highest point, watched the sunset. Vivid pink flowers jutted out of the rock.

*

When I was still in Rome, Saoli texted me to help me remember my tarot spread from the new year. She had done the Celtic Cross Spread, a multipart act of querying and receiving. The layout of the cards represented mutually enforcing phenomena centered around a single question. The question was crossed by challenge. Phenomena for 'crossing' included conscious/subconscious, past/future, hopes/fears.

I had asked—after sand and sunburn and slow wandering—something like: how am I going to move forward? The upside-down-wheel was, of course, the answer. The focus. She wrote: "This card would advise you to allow things to evolve as they should." Now, as I write, I wonder, charged by the card: what does it mean to 'allow things to evolve as they should'? There's a passivity involved, or at least detachment. Now, as I write, I wonder: can I be ambivalent and vigilant at once?

Earlier that California day, as we watched children run into the water, we reflected on the ways in which we feel reached by love. We both agreed that attention—through time, touch, conversation—was everything. I recalled a scene from years prior. Will and I were in rural Ohio. After walking through the trees all afternoon, drinking coffee and kissing in the shade, we drove to a Walmart. We didn't particularly need anything. We were bored and wanted to marvel at the excessiveness and fluorescence of the superstore. We made jokes about spreading marshmallow fluff over each other's bodies, licking it off. The plastic jars of chemical sugar were the size of my head. We laughed when a middle-aged woman overheard us—the way her face wrinkled in confusion.

I told Saoli about this scene, the absurdity of it, and said I had forgotten everything good. She said, "Maybe, now, you're ready to let go."

JANUARY 14, 2019
FROM SAOLI NASH

The spread showed that you were struggling with trying to juggle several things at once (2 of Pentacles), and while you were aware deep down that you were certainly in a fortunate and secure/stable position with both your current relationship and perhaps also your career (10 of Pentacles) your conscious mind was "stuck" on Will, perhaps in a way where rather than being appreciative of your current fortune, you're hung up on nostalgia (6 of Cups) and you're overanalyzing things in a way that's causing you some pain (Knight of Swords; a "double-edged" suit of cunning responsibility and the responsibility/anxiety that may come with it). The Moon would point to a lot of confusion, especially in the form of conflicting emotions and illusions, which can be helped by trusting your gut and following your intuition (aka trust that 10 of Pentacles) and I believe your outcome was the Wheel of Fortune in reverse (I don't remember which of the others were reverse but I remember the reversal of this card which felt significant), the reversal which implied that you were experiencing resistance to change, but "what goes around comes around" as they say, and this card would advise you to allow things to evolve as they should (and to trust that karma requires that those who have wronged you will eventually get their just desserts without your intervention). Maybe also to go further, the Knight of Swords was interpreted as a specific person in your life, as usually face cards often point to specific people (or to yourself), and the Moon and the Wheel of Fortune were Major Arcana cards that I think give information on the overall feel of the spread and can help pinpoint the querent's position in their journey based on where the Major Arcana card falls within the "Fool's Journey." (The Moon comes towards the end of the Fool's Journey at number XVIII of XXI, which implies you are likely to find clarity on your emotions soon; the Wheel is number X, which suggests that you may have to give yourself a little more time to get used to your new circumstances and not to pressure yourself to move on as quickly as you may feel obligated to (Whereas Judgment, XX, also indicates acceptance of change, but would urge you more strongly to come to some sort of decision).

*

    I kept a journal with me in Rome, burgundy with pink paper, and took notes of what I did each day. On January 14th, I started writing this essay. I heard the bells outside my apartment window when I woke at noon and couldn't leave my bed. I opened my laptop and started to write. The bedsheets in this apartment were sage green, the same color as mine in South Bend. A painting of bright red poppies on a black background hung above the bed, and a potted, viney plant draped in the window to the right of where I slept each night. Green reaching for green. Bells echoing with other bells.

*

I only want to fill this space with German Shepherds on the seashore, my grandmother combing her hair, my grandfather tending to his garden. I only want to fill this space with bells, with olive trees, with stone pines, white pillows.

*

       The wheel turns.

*

       The wheel turns.

*

The construction of the phrase "as I write, I wonder" reminds me of the unavoidable hymn: I wonder as I wander. During the summer our strain became unbearable, Will and I walked along the St. Joseph River. We walked past the dog park nearly every day on our way to see the water—for relief, for laughter, for anything. Animals running under the too-hot sun.

At some point of some walk, Will reached into his pocket, pulled out his phone, played a version of the hymn for me. He held his phone in between our heads so we could share the sound as we moved. The singer's annunciation floored me, his rhythmic destabilizing of utterance. His syncopation. I need you to listen with me.

[*I Wonder As I Wander – Carols & Love Songs* by John Jacob Niles. "I Wonder As I Wander." Two minutes, twenty-one seconds.]

In *Syncope: The Philosophy of Rapture*, Deirdre M. Mahoney and Sally O'Driscoll translate Catherine Clément's definition of syncope as "a sudden flight into nonexistent time." Examples are provided: fainting, depressive spells, hiccups, orgasms, breath. Crucially, Mahoney and O'Driscoll use the word "crossing" to emphasize the mystical site mid-binary, the "real crossing" between *before* and *after*. They translate:

> The advantage of syncope is precisely that one always returns from it. Asthmatics, epileptics, lovers—they recount explicitly how wonderful it is to breathe after the attack. [...] We place ourselves in the *before* death, in the *after* death. The real crossing is forgotten.

In "I Wonder as I Wander," if syncopation is a compulsive inhalation, what site does the song take? Where does the song take the listener, the musician? Where does syncopation transport one to? I need you to listen with me. Listen—for every pause between word, a breath. "But high from God's heaven—a stars's light did fall—and the promise—of ages—it then did recall."

Is breath-as-syncope "the real crossing"? I could notate—with em-dashes as symbols—every pause John Jacob Niles falls into during the song. And this *falling into* is crucial, the crux. Where does he go in these breaths? These are moments of divination, a human plea-as-praxis for supernatural future-telling. In *Sound: An Acoulogical Treatise*, Michel Chion writes that sound is "the coming and going where something has moved in the meantime, between the coming and going." In "I Wonder as I Wander," sound—the material of voice—finds its in-between-ness emphasized through breath.

This hymn is important to me because of the relationality it suggests. When John Jacob Niles sings "like you or like I," he elongates the vowel of the "I," the *eye*, subjectivity. in this elongation, he invites empathy, being-with. Chion describes vowels as "carriers of pitch and capable of prolongation." This "prolongation" of sound is a social invitation: to enter into the song and be with its sounds. So, as I write this book, I elongate the personal—the *eye*—in hopes that a reader feels called to participate alongside me, to envision and, ultimately, feel personal resonances, dissonances, points for interaction and departure.

*

When I think about *Syncope*, I can't help but consider the Celtic Cross tarot spread. This "real crossing" of Clément's syncope, in between the before and after death, is the crossing of the tarot spread. In this crossing: questions and suggestions, symbols for discerning. A wheel turns. What do we make of it? What symbols does it yield? What symbols does it cycle through?

And I wonder: is a syncope a difference? In *Difference and Repetition*, Paul Patton translates Gilles Deleuze to assert that "the principle of difference understood as difference in the concept does not oppose but, on the contrary, allow the greatest space possible for the apprehension of resemblances." The idea of a resemblance is the sound of a resonance. Resemblance, resonance, yields feeling. If, as Deleuze says, difference doesn't oppose resemblance, perhaps it opens space for resonance. For example, the irregular breaths of "I Wonder As I Wander," felt in part and in whole, apprehend the return from syncope. There's a certain livelihood to difference. There's a certain humanity.

Deleuze also says that "repetition is in its essence symbolic." He says that "the meeting between these two notions, difference and repetition, can no longer assumed: it must come about as a result of interferences and intersections between these two lines." Moving through the material of my memory and experiences as a site for divining, for developing a symbol set, is my way of inhabiting such "interferences and intersections."

*

I only want to fill this space with—an inhalation—*For all—of god's angels—in heaven to sing.*

*

On White Rock Mountain, Will and I walked around the circumference at sunset. We took off our clothes, laid down on the edge—over two thousand feet above sea level. We made love on the ground, smooth wet rocks under my back. Transposed just a few feet to the left, we would have rolled off the cliff, past the trees, to something bloody and unimaginable. We woke the next morning with blood-red bug bites circling our stomachs.

*

The night I wrote my song in Rome, Kelly and I went out to dinner at a restaurant I couldn't afford. It was raining, the first rain of our travels. I bought a cheap yellow umbrella from a store for tourists on my walk over to the restaurant. I don't know what we talked about over our meal. We spent hours together each day and night, wandering and drinking and talking. Time blurred and warped and bloomed—and this temporal distortion, this psychic closeness was what mattered most. We traced and retraced our steps along the Tiber, to and from Trastevere. We looked at skulls and stained glass and silk dresses and dogs and—*those trees!* I'd exclaim, not yet knowing their name. *Stone pines*, I'd learn.

After our meal, I walked back to my apartment. I can't remember the precise moment when I started singing to myself. I never sing in public, but there I was—in the rain, in Rome, under a yellow umbrella—and I was singing a song I started writing in my sleep months prior. I was singing a song, improvising it, and I kept singing it as I unlocked the door to my apartment building, and I kept singing it as I took the old elevator to the fifth floor where my room was, and I kept singing it as I entered my bedroom and the heater was on high power.

I was singing it as I took off my leather jacket and got a glass of water and sat on my bed with the sage green sheets. I recorded a voice memo on my phone, so quiet because the walls were thin, and I'd been hearing a man have violently loud sex from three in the morning until seven in the morning most nights that week. I didn't want anyone to hear me. My lips were chapped and my feet hurt from walking. I was singing a lyric that came into my head as I dreamed in October, a lyric and a melody that woke me up, that I sang to myself in half-sleep for as long as I could, trying to commit it to memory, only to find out I'd lost it by the morning. I'd lost it when I fell back asleep.

The voice memo was obscure, near-indecipherable. The tone of my whisper met dissonance in the reverberation-inducing architecture of the apartment. As I listened to it in the coming days, always coming to or going from time with Kelly, I thought about an essay I'd read about acoustic design in early European churches.[1] Sanctuaries were designed to obscure the voice of the preacher so the congregation never got a full sense of the divine word. Reverberation signified the dissonance between the divine word and a human's psychic inability to access the word. The language. Reverberation—a symbolic communication obscuring literal meaning. While there was nothing divine about the words I sang, I thought about who it might reach—how clearly, if clearly.

When I finally met with Dario to record the song, it started to rain as we walked across the street for a pre-session espresso. He looked at me and remarked, "it was raining when you wrote the song, too, and it hasn't rained since until now," remembering the significance from a conversation we had days prior.

*

The day I told Dario about the rain, we walked around Trastevere for nearly twelve hours. We drove through a tunnel of trees to a park—the park I learned about stone pines, Tree #3. We talked about times he'd been drunk in Bologna. We talked about the ways sound could be a symbol. *What does a bell mean, when you hear it? What about a telephone ringing?* We talked about traveling by boat. He wanted to return to Sardinia. We talked about walking, the way walking could be symbolic through its repetitiveness. And we talked about repetition—is it meditative, or obsessive?

I was thinking particularly about the Capuchin Crypt. Kelly and I went to the crypt during the first few days of our time in Rome, and we learned that the construction of a chapel out of bones—bones choreographed in floral patterns, baroque patterns, pelvis bones as angel wings surrounding skulls—required painstaking attention. That the monks who constructed the chapel did so in a trance. The placards in the museum said that this trance was one of joy and peace and reverence. I couldn't imagine joyfully manipulating corpses, but the effect of the bones was awesome—in the awe-inspiring sense, in the way death became art, became sacred.

Dario and I had been talking and walking for nearly six hours now, and we stopped in the middle of his favorite street when we heard a violin being played. The sounds of the violin reverberated off of the stones of the buildings surrounding us. At first, I'd noticed a carpentry shop with an industrial door wide open, light shining from inside the shop onto the cobblestone street. I smelled sawdust. We were standing side by side, our shoulders nearly touching, our minds lost in the stream of conversation—and this violinist halted us, affected pause, prolonging. At first, I thought the sounds of the violin were coming from within the carpentry shop and was delighted by the possibility. The moment I looked in front of us, the violinist was directly in our path, vigilant for no one, attending to the sounds filling our shared space.

*

When I returned from Rome, Will and I met each other in a parking lot outside of a Cracker Barrel on the Indiana-Kentucky border. We hadn't spoken in six months. I was retrieving our cat, Carrot. When I saw her in his car, I cried. What I thought would be transactional became something else. Will reached for my hand. Something else, and—the wheel turns.

The Cracker Barrel was on Killdeer Road. For years, we had been in a band called Fawn. Eventually, we got a cease and desist from an EDM artist named Fawn, a white woman with dreadlocks and a Berklee College of Music email signature. But, for the year that we were Fawn, our music took us all over the country. I remember driving from a performance at Middlebury College in Vermont to a house show in Amherst, Massachusetts—organized by a brilliant musician, Wendy Eisenberg, who we met through our friend Trish. The artwork for their record *Its Shape Is Your Touch* alchemizes tarot symbolism. The red red throne. The blue blue sky. The crosses, the hovering crown, the checkerboard floor superimposed on a valley.

I need you to listen with me.

[*Its Shape Is Your Touch* by Wendy Eisenberg.
"The Designated Mourner." Five minutes, two seconds.]

Another friend, Tevan, hosted us at Middlebury, and we slept in his loft. We smoked weed and he made us too-strong martinis and I tried to talk about via negativa while falling asleep at the kitchen table. We woke the next morning shivering—it was mid-October and the first frost of the year. After Will and I had breakfast with Tevan, we drove through the Green Mountains to Amherst, pulling off the side of the road as much as we could to inhabit the space.

Wendy was out of town when we performed—they had a performance in Boston—so they let us sleep in their bedroom. They shared a big house in the middle of nowhere, right beside a mountain, with a handful of other artists. We smoked with one of their housemates before the show and played with their house-dog, a gentle pit bull named Dandelion. It wasn't our best performance—we were exhausted from crossing half of America in just five days—but I slept like a baby that night, and when I woke I saw a copy of Chris Kraus' *Aliens & Anorexia* on Wendy's bookshelf.

I found, in this book, self-starvation as another kind of syncope, albeit one I'd never experienced explicitly. It was the first time I'd read about Simone Weil in contemporary literature and I felt like I was encountering a distant relative, an echo. Her idea of attention as the highest form of prayer was, perhaps, my first push toward vigilance. I'd written about Weil, or tried to, in a shorter hybrid text called "Reading/Grieving: a Movement in 'X' Parts." Weil's exploration of contradiction fascinated me. I was thinking about this contradiction in relation to Clarice Lispector's Água Viva, its "X" as emblem and force.** I wrote, then:

> In this space, I say "bring up" to acknowledge a bearing, an ascent (to what?). I say "bring up" —Simone Weil's mountain. In "Contradiction," the French mystic writes:
>
>> The existence of opposite virtues in the souls of saints: the metaphor of climbing corresponds to this. If I am walking on the side of a mountain I can see first a lake, then, after a few steps, a forest. I have to choose either the lake or the forest. If I want to see both lake and forest at once, I have to climb higher.
>>
>> Only the mountain does not exist. It is made of air. One cannot go up: it is necessary to be drawn.
>
> Here, Weil emphasizes perception, persistence and mental activation, the latter via the necessity "to be drawn." One senses an imperative. This mountain "made of air"—a contradiction in and of itself—is the open space of grief. Weil's anaphoric "I have to" signals spiritual compulsion, Derrida's "will to know and will to essence."
>
> I understand contradiction thusly: opposing constructs/phenomena generating deeper meaning through relationality, always held—individually and communally—with an awareness of the potentiality for cancellation, annihilation. This potential for "X" is what makes us human rather than god(s). We might be like saints—all of us—but we move forever through time upon the crossroads of "[climbing] higher" and the impossibility of ascent. The crossroads, then, signify the physical and psychic site for contradiction to manifest. The crossroads: "when the attention has revealed the contradiction in something on which it has been fixed." Attention, tension. The crossroads: site of fixedness, flowing.

*

    Will and I wrote a song about one of our stops along the Green Mountains: Texas Falls. The name was funny to us, in that nothing about Vermont recalled Texas. In the same way I noticed vivid pink flowers in Arkansas, I noticed a single yellow bloom by the water. The air was cold, the sound of the waterfall and the wind—every now and then, a speeding car down the road parallel to us—created a sonic space around our movement. We were silent as we moved, lucid, alert like deer. A lyric in the song: *space turns around our breath.*

    Outside the Cracker Barrel, I pointed Killdeer Road out to Will. I told him I didn't want to die yet. I laughed. He asked me how I was doing, and I said something about abundance. I said, honestly, that I didn't know. I shrugged in the same way my grandfather, dementia-addled, playfully gestures when I ask how he's doing. How could he know?

*

After Dario and I saw the street violinist, we shared a bottle of wine at a place a few minutes away. He knew the waiter, his friends were coming and going, all saying hi to us—whether we were smoking a cigarette outside, wine glass in hand, or seated at our table. In the same way that Saoli and I turned to talking about love, so did we. We wondered aloud: what constitutes a good stress—when a connection is 'the good work' versus when it's too too fraught. I shared some recent stresses—embodied within me as headaches, sleeplessness—the first time I'd articulated them to a friend. Not everything needs to resonate, to be relayed—not the stresses, already illuminating a turning of the wheel. His response, however, touched me. He looked at me and said: "Anne Malin, you're free."

*

In Saoli's tarot spread for me, she drew the Knight of Swords and interpreted it as a certain person in my life—according to psychicrevelation.com, a man with 'hair on the darker end of the spectrum'—who I was awaiting word from. This man possessed forceful energy, and with that energy would come clarity of some kind.

"Active meditations are useful now," the website said.

What is the relationship between active meditations and ambivalence/vigilance?

I only want to fill this space with pink flowers, with blood bloom, with blistered feet.

I only want to fill this space with white rock, clear rock, quartz rock, a clearing.

*

I only want to fill this space with white rock, clear rock, quartz rock, a clearing.

I only want to fill this space with white rock, clear rock, quartz rock, a clearing.

I only want to fill this space with white rock, clear rock, quartz rock, a clearing.

Is there actualization in repetition?

*

When Will and I met outside Cracker Barrel, the parking lot was full—Sunday brunch. I wore things my loved ones had given me like talismans: a t-shirt Amandla bought me at a dive bar in San Juan, a crucifix ring Anne bought me at an antique store in Ann Arbor, my grandmother's amber earrings. We only spoke for five minutes and were both surprised at the relief we felt to see each other. We hugged each other—the physical knowingness, of having shared nearly a decade together, was a balm to me. He told me he was thrilled I got into UC-San Diego's PhD in Literature program. I told him I was happy he was finding happiness in his life, now. That he wasn't scared to assert himself. We went our separate ways, again.

A few weeks later, Will appeared on my driveway. He had driven from Nashville to South Bend to take me out to dinner. We wanted to get to know each other after some time had passed. We wanted to be vigilant—to attend to the peace we felt on the Indiana-Kentucky border, and to expect nothing from it. After dinner, we waltzed to Elvis in a downtown dive bar. It was a Monday night, and there was only one other customer. A neon sign flickering "Hamburger Beer" was on the mildewed wall to our right. As we danced, I overheard the customer say to the bartender: "nothing romantic ever happens here." It was the first time we'd laughed in six months, one of the first times we'd danced together.

Before this surprise visit, I listened to an episode of Revisionist History on Elvis and the failure of performance. I was on the train to Chicago to see Mount Eerie and Marisa Anderson perform at the Art Institute. The last time I saw Marisa Anderson, I was with Will at Constellation. At Constellation, I had five consecutive flashbacks over the course of her hour-long performance.

Amazing Grace. Cloud Corner. Deep Gap.

Now—train-side blur. A kind of wheel, a wheeling.

The subject of the podcast, of my listening: in every live rendition of Elvis' "Are You Lonesome Tonight?", the King became a thing of sweat, blubbering under spotlights. The spoken bridge of the song, a force of vulnerability and confession, induced irreparable hysteria. A line from the bridge: "I never missed a cue." Imagine, the irony—Elvis in a white silk suit, sweating through his blouse and his briefs, crying as he forgot the words of purported infallibility.

And I'm standing there with emptiness all around.

*

    I don't know what the wheel looks like to me, how *material* it even is. I know what it looks like in my tarot deck—the Tarot of Marseille—and I know what it looks like when it makes vehicles move in Amish country in Indiana, on Coast Highway in California. According to Wikipedia, "the earliest known use of the wheel for transportation is in Mesopotamian chariots about 3200 years ago." Here, this thing of movement possesses practicality in its material form. But—what else is a force of transportation? How else can one be transported?

    I don't know how religious I am, but I know what compels me: Amazing Grace, In the Garden, I Wonder as I Wander. I don't know how religious I am, but I know what fills my breath and halts it and brings me to my knees. I'm attending to a turning thing. I'm attending to a moving thing. And what moved me more than Santa Maria in Trastevere?

    I'm back in Rome, now. I'm in my memory.

Reportedly the first church in Rome dedicated to Mary, Santa Maria in Trastevere is also—perhaps, given this trivia, necessarily—one of Rome's oldest. It dates back to the fourth century. Of all of the churches I wandered to and from in Rome over the course of seventeen days, this one was the most golden. Of all of the churches I wandered to and from in Rome, it evoked a syncope within me. What I really want to note, what I really want to uplift, are the eyes of Santa Maria.

Can the insertion of photography signal a bursting out of text? I want to perform a syncope.

I want to be floored, to write this from the floor in whispers.

Above one of the chapels in the interior is a painting of disembodied eyes, guarded by a golden frame, a hovering crown. Is the space between the frame and the crown a breath, a suspension, a site for syncope? What I do know is that these eyes are a visual difference within the space of the sanctuary. The strike you from afar, they follow you, they know something you don't.

When Will and I performed in New Orleans in May 2018, I got a tattoo on my collarbone an hour before our show. I had re-read Gaston Bachelard's *The Poetics of Space* at Watermill, another reprieve from the arduous gardening, and was struck by his invocation of Rimbaud's "nacre voit"—*mother-of-pearl sees*. I emailed one of my favorite contemporary fashion designers, Claire Barrow, asking if she'd handwrite the phrase for me. She replied within a week.

We performed at Saturn Bar in an old fighting ring lit by a red spotlight. A dilapidated balcony, where onlookers once watched bodies beat to bruising, to blood, served as a site for listening. After a year of touring, we'd accidentally developed this performance style of pacing—while Will played guitar and I sang—making unwavering eye contact. Like bulls in a ring.

I find "nacre voit" in the eyes of Santa Maria. The eyes, to me, signal the dissonance designed into early European churches, but this time visual; the eyes beg the question— what aren't you seeing clearly? This time, however, the eyes suggest a femininity. A mother—a divine mother—is asking, inviting clearer perception.

Dario's recording studio was a block away from Santa Maria, yet he'd never been in it before. On our long day of wandering, I told him he had to be in the space. When he saw the eyes, he stopped and asked me: "what do you think they're looking at?"

NACRE VOIT

NACRE VOIT

NACRE VOIT

Nacre Voit

*

    There are reasons why I love sleep and reasons why I hate forgetting. I was diagnosed with PTSD a year into my relationship with Will—after losing my appetite, losing fifteen pounds, and blacking out when I saw certain men on my college campus or around Boston or Allston or Cambridge. To complicate the geography further, I was diagnosed by my therapist over Skype while I was studying abroad in Dublin. That spring, I listened to Elvis' "In the Garden" on repeat every day, starved and disassociated. So, when I say I don't *know* the syncope of anorexia, thinking of Kraus and of Weil, I never intended for that kind of starvation—and yet. I wrote a poem about it, 'Via Negativa'—

Sound the O,
                    mouth-hollow
        echo
                          past self
                                      Rose-
                                      blood
                                tongue
                        I faint
                into negative space
        neither forward
                              nor back
Hollowing echo,
        herald
                of This
                          what I don't
                    see:
                (don't I
        intersect
                      light?)
                          My hours
                                gut-wounded
    on a bus
                    listening
                on loop—
                          I come
                      to the garden
                  alone
                      come
          bone-spent
                    beside the river
My diachronic being
                falling into
                                            noth-
ing:
                                    dreams woken
                        up from
              by halo of sweat

```
                Mouth
                                        cavernous,
                                                        mute
        O come O
                        come
                                        being
up water-
fall up
                ancient grave
                                        holding self
                                                                out
                                over lake,
                                                        receptacle,
        my memory
                        receiver
                                Crossing
                                                        moon
                                over bridge
                        Crossing
psychic un-
        fainting
        through
                        morning rain
                                                Green's fevered
                                                sprawl
                                        Un-sweat
                        of dew
                                                If I could
                                                drink
        (don't I
drink it?)
```

*

My mother visited me right before my diagnosis. We took a car to Connemara, drove around in the country with a kind old Irish man, stopped to look at the Connemara ponies on the hillside. Stopped to look at grottos and roadside shrines. I had always been interested in—or compelled by—Marian symbolism, and Connemara's roadsides offered shrines to the female martyr. Ironically, the experiences of my traumas circled around a desire to heal other men, to give them the benefit of the doubt—one a drug addict who sexually assaulted and emotionally abused me, another who raped me. For a time, I was focusing on healing together—which often mutated, with or without my consent—versus nurturing my own solidity.

In W. B. Yeats' "Symbolism and Poetry," he writes:

> The purpose of rhythm, it has always seemed to me, is to prolong the moment of contemplation, the moment when we are both asleep and awake, which is the one moment of creation, by hushing us with an alluring monotony, while it holds us waking by variety, to keep us in that state of perhaps real trance, in which the mind liberated from the pressure of the will is unfolded in symbols.

One of the most exciting poetry readings I went to was in Greenough, Montana, at a retreat organized by my friend and mentor Chris Dombrowski. I can't remember the name of the writer, and I think that's the point. For thirty minutes, the writer read interconnected quotes from his favorite authors. He didn't share any of his own work—his work was this connection-making. More than post-hermeneutic, it felt human. I wonder: does the site of the essay afford the same humanity? At some point, raising attention to external passages and moving around the wheel with them risks arbitrariness, unfixed-ness. I want solidity within these movements, these movements-as-connection.

Are you with me?

I turn back to Yeats: in this passage, sound is given a psychic capacity. Rhythm—as with John Jacob Niles—opens space. Re-listening to "I Wonder As I Wander," and bearing Yeats' assertions in mind, these breaths invite the listener's contemplation in the same way that the elongated vowels—the "I"-as-*eye*—do. These breaths and moments of elongation comprise the rhythm of the performance. Yeats' turn to "hushing" may be, again, that of syncope; this "hushing" inhabits a site of in-between-ness. For Yeats, this in-between-ness is not before and after death, but a moment of impossibility: "we are both asleep and awake." It is in this site of in-between-ness that symbols appear, apparitions.

Will visited me in Dublin after my diagnosis and we went to the Yeats Archive. We talked about *A Vision* and the occult. We walked by the Liffey and found this incredible restaurant run by Hari Krishnaists, Govinda's, where we ate and ate. We listened to fiddles and guitars and the sounds of traffic. We made love in the Castle Hotel, walked through its winding and narrow hallways steering each other with our bodies.

*

I only want to fill this space with narrow hallways in Dublin as the slope of the wheel, waterfalls in Vermont as the slope of the wheel, the moment two distant hands touch, skin rough, veins pulsing.

*

    In *Difference and Repetition*, I find myself bewildered. Deleuze writes: "forgetting becomes a positive power while the unconscious becomes a positive and superior unconscious." After spending five years remembering and recollecting and combing through my past, could I find my being change through forgetfulness? Could I not be ashamed of my memory?

*

After Watermill, I had dreams about Giovanni. These dreams usually coincided with choreographies—wherein I'm backstage at a dance performance, or he's acting onstage, or I'm trying on a costume and aware of his presence nearby. I felt guilty about these dreams; I didn't know how to make sense of them, how they fit into my actual relationship. As a former dancer, it was mystifying to be in spaces of performance again, and in my sleep. I loved the feeling of swaying, of light hitting my arm, of breathing as I pushed my body through space. In reality, my body was motionless in bed, my breath slow. Whenever I saw Giovanni after these imagined performances, we'd be in tight spaces, people moving all around us, only able to talk for a minute.

Another recurring dream involved descending a narrow staircase, usually spiraling, to a room with beige-white marble walls. There would be other people with us, often friends from Watermill. They shared glasses of red wine and talked about scenography. Notebook paper with architectural drawings and a collection of sculptures were always nearby. In these dreams, I always felt a sense of anticipation as I descended the stairwell in solitude, knowing (especially as the dream became regular) who I would see when I stepped off of the lowest stair. Again, we rarely had time to talk. In retrospect, the dream seemed more about the feelings of anticipation and passion I felt as I walked down the stairs, and the impossibility of an encounter..

(Voice it again: *setting-as-catalyst*.)

I'm thinking about Alice Notley's *The Descent of Alette*, a feminist epic with a choreography inherent in its very name. I'm thinking about how *Purgatorio* wheels and *Alette*-as-poem and Alette-as-character descend. The more Alette descends in the book, the more emotional significance is attributed to the act (or force) of descent. Each downward movement requires vigilance towards one's interiority; each downward movement becomes increasingly destabilizing and vital to the character's—and her world's—healing.

While Alette materializes in a subway system—already underground—she moves further and further down throughout the poem, into more mystical and mystifying geographies. She is aware of a man called the Tyrant who controls the space she inhabits. Notley defends the choreography of *Alette* in her essay "The Feminist Epic," noting that the movement of the poem defies the "male tradition". While following tropes of Dante's *Inferno*, Notley "deliberately reversed the Dantean, Christian, and other religious direction of 'enlightenment,' making it a descent into darkness." Ultimately, through a tarot-like card game involving roses and black panthers, Alette learns that she must kill the Tyrant. This poem-within-epic-poem goes:

"'We will draw cards,' I said," "'for who does it" "The one who

draws'" "the highest card" "performs the act" "The man handed me" "a deck of cards" "It contained" "the two suits of" "roses" "& panthers" "Red roses &" "black panthers" "'Which is the higher suit?'" "someone asked" "'The highest suit" "is a third suit"

"always,' I said," "'& this deck" "contains that suit:" "the composite suit," "roses/panthers," "half & half'" "Then I myself "drew the highest card," "the ace of" "roses/panthers" " I will do it,' I said" "'You want me, don't you," "to kill the tyrant?"

"I will kill him" "but it won't happen" "quite yet" "I have to journey first" "farther down" "into this darkness'"

*

    Keats died in Rome. This much I knew. I walked past the Spanish Steps several times during my time abroad as tourists with Gucci bags and cameras swarmed the sun-lit stone descent. I passed the Keats-Shelley house, imagining pulses of the poet's meter reaching from distant architectures to my body. I imagined sound turning around my legs, gripping my thighs, holding me onto the earth. I didn't want to see the actual site of Keats' burial, preferring to sense his ambiguous posthumous proximity with every step I took. I didn't want to see the interior of the house. I knew Keats died young, at twenty-five, that he was sent away from home for the Roman air. The air: a kind of medicine. Apparently ten thousand books were housed beside the Spanish Steps. What did Keats listen to as his pulse slowed? Did it slow, even? Did anyone read to him? And if they read, at what pace? When Will first moved out, I read and re-read "Ode to a Nightengale." Later, I'd record it as a voicemail and send it to him through space.

*

The wheel turns.

*

The wheel turns.

*

On a Thursday night in March, Anne called to tell me that Tag committed suicide. Anne, Tag and I grew up spending our summers in northern Michigan, a small town on the lake called Petoskey. We'd known each other since we were five years old. When I was fourteen, I had a crush on Tag, but was flushed, paralyzed, mute. In high school, Tag was an athlete, and seemed to have escaped the physical manifestations of pubescent awkwardness. They were lithe, graceful, silly. The July sun tanned their skin to a dark gold color, their curly hair made blonder by the light. I was a dancer, still, at that time, and admired how muscular their legs were. Tag was a kind of profane angel—someone Keats or Blake might write about. A running figure on a Grecian Urn.

Anne, on the other hand, stayed close to me, a sister. Nearly every night, every summer, she'd come to my family's cottage to drink chamomile tea in our wood-paneled kitchen at dusk. The sound of the lake was barely audible from outside. We talked freely about our dreams, our relationships to ourselves and to others. We talked about love and hurt—a decade's worth. As these conversations became routine, we both took them for granted. After Tag's death, though, we realized the vitality of these conversations, constantly evolving as we grew older. We grew near-fluent in each other's anxieties and excitements. Anne told me that talking to me was like writing in a diary, a space both deep and unafraid.

I always felt a sense of relief arriving at my family's cottage. It rested at the bottom of a steep hill and was on the lake. Our lawn was unkempt, one large tree stood in its midst, and my mother's gardening brought an array of blooms and fragrances into the disorder: bleeding hearts, hydrangeas, lavender. We kept a small garage separate from the cottage, housing paddle boards, a metal canoe and a handful of bicycles. Every day, I'd bike from my cottage to East Park and back. East Park stood on a bluff overlooking Lake Michigan, and the bike path that connected my cottage to its slope stayed close to the lake the entire way. Smells of wildflowers and stone and seaweed wafted in the breeze, nearly indecipherable but a perfume I came to recognize as my own.

Relief: the moment I reached the top of my family's street, stopped pedaling, and coaxed the brake as I sped down the hill to turn onto our driveway. Wind in my hair, whirring in my ears—as if to fill me, to propel me home.

*

By the time I was eighteen, Tag noticed me. I had just graduated high school and was a few months out of an abusive relationship. I'm not sure how Tag and I came together, in what precise moment, but one night in early summer, Anne, our friend Alexina and I were sending Tag adolescent text messages from behind the safety of a tree near their driveway. I had initiated this tree-hiding text-mission, clueless as to confidence. Eventually, they snuck outside with a lilting smile to tell us they were grounded.

The time I spent with Tag was always surrounded by trees or by the water. I had recently acquired a hammock, and we hung it in the woods at sunset, tucked away where no one would find us, to kiss each other and talk. We smoked weed out of a crushed soda can and talked about Devendra Banhart's song "Michigan State." We never talked about what would happen after the summer, but I missed them terribly as I moved to Boston to start college. I didn't want our connection to end and didn't know how to say that. They made me a mix CD when we said goodbye. I remember "Michigan State." I remember the Velvet Underground's "Satellite of Love" and Yo La Tengo's "Today Is the Day."

In the wake of Tag's death, I listened to "Today Is the Day" on loop. The song sounds like peaceful nothingness on the beach. Its gentle percussion, fluid voice, reverberant pseudo-slide-guitar. It recounts memories of togetherness, and while Tag and I never did what the song says, I could feel ourselves in its movements: *I followed you foolishly*. In the wake of Tag's death, I walked around South Bend aimlessly, haunted, wearing all black clothes and black cat-eye sunglasses. I cut my hair short again, like it was when we were together. When the hairdresser massaged my scalp before cutting my hair, I closed my eyes. I focused on the heat of the water on my skull, trying not to cry. On my walk home, hair dry, I wept.

*

    Within the same week of Tag's suicide, the poet W. S. Merwin died. Grief-struck, I looked through old photos. To get back to 2013, the year Tag and I dated, I passed through photos of Rome, Corona del Mar, South Bend. I stopped upon seeing a photo from July 2017, right before I went to Watermill. Will and I were celebrating our last day together in Boston, and we went to the Arboretum. I took a photo of a tree trunk, a metal tag affixed to its bark, because I was struck by its name: Form of the Tree of Heaven.

    Tag and I lost touch after our shared summer, but closer to their death they had an internship at the National Arboretum. I saw some of their sketches of bonsai trees on Instagram. Tag was an artist and was studying ceramics at a university in Ohio. After their death, Anne told me she had been watching videos about ceramics online, trying to better feel Tag's presence. Trying to understand. Anne was able to go to Tag's memorial service and told me that all of Tag's ceramics were on display. She said it was beautiful, like they were in the room with her—still breathing, smiling.

    W. S. Merwin had a nature conservatory in Hawaii, where he lived with his wife. I read about it in *The Paris Review*'s Art of Poetry feature and, upon seeing a portrait of the poet, was haunted by the similarities between Merwin's eyes and Tag's eyes. Blue, bright. The interviewer for *The Paris Review* described Merwin's eyes as "intensely clear." In the interview, Merwin described poetry as "an attempt to use language as completely as possible." Poetry is a way of recognizing connection, he said. I pictured Merwin reciting poetry surrounded by papaya trees. His voice beside palms, gardenias, ferns. I pictured those eyes—connective, clear, a force beyond life.

*

I only want to fill this space with Tag, crouched beside a bonsai, ink pen in hand.

I only want to fill this space—Form of the Tree of Heaven.

*

When I told Saoli about Tag's suicide, she recommended I do a tarot spread specifically meant for grief. I only wanted to do it from the floor of Santa Maria, the frame-suspended eyes watching my palms on paper, my shins pressed to the tile floor as I bent toward the cards on my knees. I only wanted the eyes to be a site where Tag could see me from—to see me pray for them. I wanted Tag to know how they haunted me—how, for months at night, I'd walk in my closet and imagine their face beside my dresses. In the years we didn't speak, I lost all proximity to Tag's vision. I saw what they made out of clay from the distant screen of my phone. I saw the glaze on ceramics: blue, yellow, black. When I reached out to Tag's best friend after their death, I asked what had excited them recently. Even a year before their death. Even something small. I never heard back.

*

A month after Tag's death, I dreamed I was walking across Petoskey to get to a summertime memorial service. I was wearing bright colors, the sun was blinding, and the breeze from the lake reached the path I walked on, curling around my ears. As I walked, weeping as I did in my waking hours, I passed Tag's mother walking to their service. Tag was walking, alive, by her side.

*

I need you to listen with me.

*

"Satellite of Love" was a seemingly innocuous song throughout my college years, so much so that I forgot its Tag-resonance when I arrived at Watermill. The annual gala I prepared for alongside my friends was in honor of Lou Reed. After performing, I sipped on a bourbon while listening to "Satellite of Love" projected through the trees. Laurie Anderson, Reed's partner, performed. I wrote about the performance in "Notes from the Eclipse," haunted by the way she played electric violin over recordings of Reed's voice, by the way she demanded tenderness with an age-roughed voice. She was conjuring a ghost. She was rendering him—sonic apparition. I didn't realize Tag had introduced me to the song until after their death, as I dug around for the CD. A hand-drawn burning spiral sun on its cover.

This Satellite, a kind of wheel. Satellite of Love. Tree of Heaven.

I wrote a poem about being in the woods with Tag. I wrote it over the course of three hours, right before my haircut, listening to Devendra Banhart's "My Dearest Friend" on loop. I hadn't listened to his music since college and felt eighteen all over again as I listened. I felt eighteen all over again as I grieved—bewildered, desirous of connection, a current of panic in my chest. When I found out Tag was interested in me, all those years ago, I was delighted. It was the first uplifting relationship I'd ever been in, the first time I found humor in attraction. After writing the poem, I learned that the earliest use of the wheel—beyond that of transportation—was for ceramics.

your certain hands   thin and   fast your   running
through   the trees   you were   pine   a memory

you were   memory   I never had   to worry   you
were song   held under   the water   you were   a song

first   quiver of   breath first   quiver of breath   your
certain   body   of sinews   certain   hair of

sheep's curl   tan stretch   of abdomen   while you danced
when everyone was   watching   first warmth   first

warmth   I never thought   of you at dawn   I never held
you when I knew   what it meant   and now   I wake and

your   smile hovers   like a ghost   next to my mouth
like a ghost   next to my mouth   and I need   a glass of

water   and green sheets   green trees   we heard trumpets
echoing from   across town   into the woods   we heard

trumpets   and wondered   for a mile   where they came
from   and now   your smile   your certain smile   like

you'd   jumped   through a mirror   when no one was
watching   and now   a pained expression   a pain

when no one was   watching   ceramic eyes   ceramic necks
trumpets through   the trees   and your body   on mine

beside the water   before I knew   what it meant   when we
were young   ceramic spiral   you shaped   a coin

you shaped   a coin   it hung above   your heart
your heart   on a leather cord

MARCH 1, 2019
FROM ERIC RINGWALT (DAD)

Kurt had a congenital heart defect called tetralogy of fallot. It's actually four different abnormalities within the heart including abnormal connections between the two larger chambers. The heart defects caused blood to bypass his lungs so basically he was not getting enough oxygen into his blood. He was diagnosed shortly after birth. Often children with this turn a bluish color due to the lack of oxygen. I know he lived longer than he was expected to and sadly it's a condition that is now corrected with surgery. I don't remember him very well. I think my sister remembers him much more than I do. I have a memory from when I was around four-years-old of an ambulance coming to the house and big green oxygen tanks.

*

On Christmas Eve in California, my grandmother gave my little brother, Kurt, a miniature basket full of miniature seashells. The name *Kurt* was painted onto the side of the basket. Something small for a baby boy. That boy, my brother's namesake, never grew up. He was my dad's younger brother and he died within his first two years of life. He hovered above our family as a reminder of innocence, of softness, of tragedy. His portrait, black-and-white, stood on a bookshelf in the foyer of my grandparents' house, held in a silver frame.

In quiet moments alone with me, my grandmother sometimes talked about the aftermath of Kurt's death. She said she'd sit in their garage in silence, petting their German Shephard. She said she couldn't have made it through the loss without the family dog. My grandmother, not one to talk about her feelings in depth, possessed a deep well of being. I could feel it whenever I sat with her. On the surface of this well was an electrical current of anxiety. I could feel that, too. Later, I learned that my grandmother's therapist told her to move on from the death, to try to forget it. I'm sure there's more to the story, but the relative silence surrounding Kurt's death was amplified by anxiety.

When my grandmother told me about holding me as a baby, she said that she felt a special connection with me. She said I was the calmest baby she'd ever held, something I find hard to imagine given my childhood—feverish, wildly imaginative. She always fostered my creativity—and my brothers', and my cousin's. I grew up dancing, playing cello, and writing stories and poems. Kurt played the drums. Daniel, our older brother, was a pianist. Heather, our cousin, was a ballerina and an actress. We all possessed degrees of the intensity of our grandmother's feeling and the strangeness of our grandfather's humor, their shared love for art.

Marjorie, our grandmother, was one of the first women to study music therapy in the United States. She moved from rural Iowa to Chicago to study at Roosevelt University, and eventually moved again to San Francisco, where she met my grandfather. Their first date was at the opening night of the San Francisco Opera. Once they married and settled into their house in Corona del Mar (which they moved to after Kurt's death in Claremont), she became a private piano instructor. She still receives letters from former students, well into her eighties.

The day I left for Rome, I was alone with my grandparents at their house. They were listening to the radio, as always, classical music flooding through the living room along with the sun. I felt painfully aware of their old age. Saying goodbye meant not knowing when I'd see them next. As I got into the taxi to John Wayne Airport, my tears transformed in gratitude as I heard the taxi driver had another classical radio station on. I commented on the music, and he told me he was an opera singer. I talked to him about my grandmother, and how I was a musician too, and he said something like music elongates life. Music gives age grace.

*

The translation of *Purgatorio* I studied in Rome was by W. S. Merwin. Once, when my grandfather was in the hospital after breaking his hip, he said to my father: "The Divine Comedy." The magic of my grandfather's speech is that I never know what valence he intends. Was he thinking about Dante? Was he calling old age or hospitalization a circle of hell? Was he dreaming of Beatrice, a mountain? When he was lucid, I think he was aware of this discrepancy—the potential for sarcasm or sincerity, or both.

Caught up in my travels, it wasn't until I got to Rome that I realized I would be skipping *Inferno* altogether. I was instantly captivated by Merwin's translation, the suggestion of *Purgatorio* as an earthly site. In his foreword to the book, Merwin writes: "Of the three sections of the poem, only *Purgatorio* happens *on* the earth, as our lives do, with our feet on the ground, crossing a beach, climbing a mountain." He goes on to explain how hope is a vital emotional element of *Purgatorio*—Dante had circled through hell and was looking, now, up.

In a way, it made sense to begin in the middle. Thinking of the Celtic Cross spread, of syncope, *Purgatorio* also possesses an in-between-ness in its very being. How does listening change when one enters into the scene in flux? In other words: what does listening to a turning wheel look like, feel like? Again, I turn—I re-turn—to tarot, to the Wheel's invitation to 'allow things to evolve as they should'. Again, I turn—I re-turn—to vigilance. One can only get their bearings in the flux, because of its movements. Setting-as-catalyst.

In Merwin's foreword, too, I find a form for feeling. He writes: "One of the first vast differences between Hell, the region of immutable despair, and Purgatory is that the latter place, when we step out on it, is earth again, the ground of our waking lives. We are standing on the earth under the sky, and Purgatory begins with a great welling of recognition and relief." I'd like to attend to the word welling. Why *welling*—why not swelling? The latter suggests a kind of overflow, a sensual surpassing of limits. The former, on the other hand, suggests vigilance in its holding of the emotional material. Swelling is usually out of one's control.

When I wept for Tag, I overflowed, I swelled. I lost myself, I was in between my body and a syncope. However, as the days passed and I knew what my terrain was—that inconsolable ache—I could hold it, embody it. I had a bodily structure—a well—to contain it. Vigilance requires awareness of a subject, an occasion, a phenomenon. With Merwin, I stand and I well, endeavoring to sustain a site for my very being.

*

I only want to fill this space with well water, lake water, the sound of a voice reverberating on its waves, into its structure.

*

Kurt Warren Ringwalt, my ghost of an uncle, lived from February 26, 1968 to October 11, 1969. Blake's "Cradle Song" is carved on his gravestone, chosen by my grandfather—

Sweet dreams, form a shade o'er my lovely infant's head.

When he was lucid, my grandfather had memorized most of Blake's poetry. He won an award for playwriting as an undergraduate at Princeton and wrote his thesis on Yeats' theater. Throughout my childhood, and into my teenage years and adulthood, he'd recite lines from poems, conjuring verse out of the air. I remember him reciting lines from T. S. Eliot's *The Wasteland* while I sat on his lap, twelve-years-old:

> "That corpse you planted last year in your garden,
> "Has it begun to sprout? Will it bloom this year?
> "Or has the sudden frost disturbed its bed?
> "Oh keep the Dog far hence, that's friend to men,
> "Or with his nails he'll dig it up again!
> "You! hypocrite lecteur!—mon semblable,—mon frère!"

As my grandfather began losing his memory, my family realized he retained his long-term memory while suffering significant short-term loss. He could recount, in full detail, climbing up Mount Fuji when he and his sister Louise lived in Japan. He talked about stopping for rice before the ascent. He talked about accidentally going AWOL while volunteering in Berlin during the Cold War. He asked my grandmother questions about distant friends and family, and he always remembered the essentials of my brothers and cousin, and myself.

I didn't know much about my grandfather's family. His mother, Anna, fled France around the time of World War II. She traveled alone to Oakland to meet up with her sisters and worked at a laundromat. My father told me that whenever he asked Anna about her time in France, she'd freeze. Silence willed fact into oblivion. In my own research, I learned that Anna's great-grandfather was a construction worker on the Eiffel Tower. I learned that the Eiffel Tower was finished being built on March 31, my birthday. While my grandfather moved across the country and across the world during his childhood as a consequence of his father's military work, he found his way back to California.

During the pre-Rome trip to Corona del Mar, I sat in the living room with my grandfather. The sun shone through the olive tree's branches and reached through the glass sliding-door to their small front porch. For the first time in my life, I read him Blake. I knew he wouldn't remember the poem after I recited it, but I felt him nodding along to the rhythm, an echo of recognition. The poem was called "Song"—

> Memory, hither come,
>   And tune your merry notes;
> And, while upon the wind,
>   Your music floats,
> I'll pore upon the stream,
>   Where sighing lovers dream,
> And fish for fancies as they pass
>   Within the watery glass.
>
> I'll drink of the clear stream,
>   And hear the linnet's song;
> And there I'll lie and dream
>   The day along:
> And, when night comes, I'll go
>   To places fit for woe,
> Walking along the darken'd valley,
>   With silent Melancholy.

*

On that same trip, my grandmother rested on the couch for her midday nap. Classical music played from the radio in an empty room down the hall. My cousin Heather and I woke her to wish her a happy new year—we had plans to spend the night in Anaheim and Orange and promised our grandmother we'd take photographs to share with her. Our grandmother had a near-obsessive fixation with photographs. She was our grandfather's primary caretaker and sat day-in and day-out with him in the living room, revisiting photographs from decade's past. She told me that these images—of travels and friendship and family—made her feel free.

When she woke from her nap, she looked innocent, bemused—as if she was waking from a dream of her youth. Despite her wrinkled skin and age-thinned frame, she looked at us with the eyes of a child. She said to us: "We Ringwalt women like to be disturbed." In this moment, our grandfather's humor seeped into her speech. While she meant that our act of waking her was a positive disturbance, Heather and I laughed about its other valences as we drove from Corona del Mar to Anaheim. We knew, after all, what anxiety pulsed under the surface. What other disturbances our family tended to.

*

The summer Will and I started dating, he visited me in Petoskey. An hour or so north of the boarding school we met at, the scene was familiar enough to echo us at sixteen, seventeen, eighteen. We hadn't seen each other in two years. The night before he arrived, a thunderstorm struck over the water. One of my best friends from our boarding school, Megan, called me to say she had a feeling something in my life was about to change. When he arrived on my street, I watched him drive down the hill to the lake, and my driveway, from out the kitchen window.

Will only visited for three days, and we spent our time at the state park on sand dunes, sailing with the patriarch of my neighbor's family, a sixty-something year-old man who had been friends with my mom's parents, and walking through the same woods I walked through with Tag. On his last night, we each had a glass of bourbon by the lake and wandered from sunset to dusk. I didn't think he'd want to be in a long-distance relationship; at twenty, I wasn't convinced that a man would stick around if I was physically unavailable. After all, I lived in Massachusetts, he lived in Ohio, and I'd be in Ireland soon.

Will told me that, the way he saw it, we'd be together for so long that one semester wouldn't change anything. He wanted to be my partner. He wanted to visit me in Dublin. He wanted to write music together. He wanted to come back to Petoskey in a few weeks and return to Interlochen—our former boarding school—together. So, as we walked through the woods, we stopped on a boardwalk over mud, laid down, and held each other in the dark. Fireflies circled overhead.

In late July, we drove an hour south to Interlochen. We walked around our former campus, listened to musicians practicing in the woods, and mused that younger versions of ourselves would be bewildered to know we were together after years of desire. We had plans to spend the night in Traverse City, just outside of the tiny town of Interlochen. When we pulled up to our motel, my gut inverted. Across the street from where we'd stay was the motel my first boyfriend assaulted me at. I didn't say anything.

When Will and I checked into the motel, we were greeted by an overly enthusiastic middle-aged woman who said something emphatic like: "Oh, you two are going to have a great night." When we opened the door to the room, I collapsed on the floor laughing. A giant heart-shaped bathtub was in our room, surrounded by mirrors.

The cruel irony of this motel-proximity was that, just a few months before Will and I reconnected, I had been raped at college, a truth I wouldn't accept until after our third anniversary—and over a year after my diagnosis. Will and I put our bags down in the room, had sex for the first time as a couple, and took a shower together. We were saving the bathtub for after dinner. I don't remember anything about our first time. I was somewhere else, and Will knew it.

We got dressed and drove to Wilson's Antiques, my favorite place to go as a teenager. The shop, with four stories of second-hand-sprawl, was a barely organized labyrinth of wooden furniture, wool sweaters, leather Victorian boots, costume jewelry, pearls in display cases, old postcards. As a teenager, I liked going to Wilson's to listen to the crystalline percussion of the rotating jewelry displays.

In the parking garage, I mustered up the courage to tell Will what was going on. I said, simply, "Something bad happened across the street from our motel." Either language or knowing failed me. He asked if we should move somewhere else for the night, and I said no, that would be a waste of money. I'd already seen the Knight's Inn, the memories were already echoing, I'd be fine. We tried on women's fur jackets—I wore a baby-pink one and Will wore a mink one. We dug through old records and family portraits. I took a photo of Will next to a framed print advertising toilet paper. He held the frame with a smirk, surrounded by old wooden furniture and small wall-mounted mirrors.

I was going to lose my virginity at the Knight's Inn. I didn't know that my then-boyfriend was using again. I didn't know that he was on the way to flunk out of high school. Last I heard, he'd taken ecstasy at eight in the morning before class. I knew he had a problem with opiates. When I met him at a summer camp at fifteen, he was going through withdrawal. He'd take anything to incapacitate himself. Still, I found myself under his body, undressing, too-thin from all of the drugs, my heart pounding. I was supposed to take off my skirt. I was supposed to unhook my bra.

All of my friends from high school had already had sex, and while their experiences were horrible at best and near-abusive at worst, they acted like it was no big deal. They encouraged me to empower myself. I didn't even want to have sex—if I had been more self-aware, I would have known that my body was actively resisting the relationship I was in. That I should run, fast.

In the year of our relationship leading up to my assault, my then-boyfriend confided in me that he was afraid his ten-year-old brother was going to stab him to death in his sleep. He told me he wanted to die—usually by way of text, when I was already sleeping—and would disappear, strung out, for days on end. Usually, he'd disappear on Sunday nights. I had a dance class on Monday afternoons, and would roll across the linoleum floor to the sound of a piano not knowing where my first love was, what my first love was on, whether or not I'd hear his voice again. Whether or not he wanted me to. This disappearing act happened several times, each as painful as the last.

In the motel bed, he put on a condom. I hadn't even touched him. Right before it could have happened, I said I changed my mind. I rolled out from under him, trying to catch my breath. I don't know how much time passed between that and his tongue, but I felt trapped in that motel room. I had no way of getting home and I felt like I owed him something. So, he put his tongue on me. He kept going. I didn't feel anything. It would come back to me in waves, knife-sharp. I'm still not sure he knew what he did, and that oblivion, that oversight—to me—made it worse. I was a body. I loved.

At school after the motel-night, as Kelly and I put on our pink tights and leotards for our dance class, I lied and told my friends in the locker room that I'd had sex. I even lied about in a chapbook I had published, *Like Cleopatra*. Years later, in a strange bed in Boston, one of my friends raped me while I was blacked out from drinking too much. He texted with another friend of ours right before I passed out—wholly aware of my vulnerability, cruelly unaware of my fearfulness. The next day, the man who did it tried to convince me I was consenting because I had feelings for him. We walked through the snow in the Theater District and talked about a song, as if nothing had happened—neither violence nor intimacy. He said it like it was true: *nothing happened*. For a while, I believed him. This, after all, was the first time I had sex—if I can call it that.

For a while, I was dying, cruelly unaware. Time-stunted, the pain brought me back to my body, woke me up.

I. motel

> *I wake you, stone. Love this man.*
> CHARLES OLSON, "THE DISTANCES"

After you set your button-down on the bed for me and I rose to my knees to kiss you, after we made love, we watched a movie about Gandhi and ate pizza in bed. Without your glasses on, you thought Gandhi was Hitler. Half-blind, I wondered what I looked like to you. I pointed this out: the last time I tried to turn you on, you were watching *Rosemary's Baby*.

The fan running in the bathroom still, the light also on.

The way our shoes rested on the floor.

*

My first boyfriend was from Pittsburgh. My older brother studied computer science at Carnegie Mellon and I wanted to push through my panic to attend his graduation. Luckily, my grandparents would be there too. The moment my family arrived at our hotel, and we made sure my grandparents were comfortable in their hotel room, I broke down. My legs went numb, my lips trembled, I cried as if to abject the abuse. Nothing was enough. I took a too-hot shower to change my body temperature, something that had often calmed me in the past.

The next morning, we drove across Pittsburgh with my brother to go to his favorite restaurant. I sat in the back row of the car with my grandfather. I asked him if I could hold his hand. He probably thought I was just being affectionate, but I was trying to survive. I closed my eyes and focused on the feel of his hand in mine, its warmth, slow pulse of blood in veins, skin softening around bone. I envisioned all that my grandfather has held in his life, and all that he forgot. I closed my eyes. I closed my eyes. Later, I'd write a poem. 'What She Inherited'. I wrote—*memory, like a knife jutting out of fog.*

*

What is a question that has stayed with you through time, clung to you like an inhalation?

What is a question that pulls you out from syncope? For me, it follows: *what does it feel like to be in the stream?* If I were always at peace, my wheel would be made from this stream.

> *I'll drink of the clear stream,*
> *And hear the linnet's song;*
> *And there I'll lie and dream*
> *The day along:*

Blake wrote that. I read that. I transcribed it, again, here.

*

The stream: my site of welling. The stream: my ideal wheeling.

*

To be in the stream. It means to be, to breathe, to drink a glass of water. To ride a bicycle down the hill, to stop and feel the wind before hitting the lake, to turn home. But I can't always be fluid, forward. I have to look back. I have to go down. I have to wheel. I have to move through my memory, or it will make itself known. A hand reaching out from the water, bloodied and raw.

I re-turn to an epigraph, to Dante. I say it aloud. "We were climbing through a fissure in the stone / that kept turning from one side to the other / as a wave that flows out and runs in again." This is how the wheel moves, upside-down.

*

I see myself in these movements. *Like you or like I—*

*

The wheel turns.

*

The wheel turns.

*

    Tarot, once for entertainment and then for esoterism, is how I want my wheel to be. I want to laugh and I want to weep. I want simultaneity-as-resonance. I want this form to be at once playful and grave. Who else draws a card when I do? Who else breathes when I do?

*

    A few months after Will moved out, I found myself sitting across the thighs of a new man, my arms and legs wrapped around him, our faces close to each other in the dim light. He stared at me for minutes, dark eyes tracing my face. We were silent. I hadn't felt watched with amazement in months. In that moment, I felt a space opening. I wanted to rest, I wanted to rest in that space, and I wanted that rest to be with him. He slept with me three nights in a row. He held me as I dreamed.

    When Saoli read my tarot spread, this was the new relationship she mentioned. N. and I first connected on a camping trip to the Indiana Dunes with a group of mutual friends. As the night drew on, I realized we'd been talking alone for hours. At four in the morning, the moon was still bright in the sky. One of our friends was on shrooms and took a photo of the two of us standing under the light of the moon, as if they'd noticed something we couldn't see ourselves. I leaned close, my hand pressing on N.'s back. As it turned out, it was too dark to see anything—not even the moon, not even moonlight on our cheekbones. It was a photo of complete blackness.

    The next day, we drove to an antique mall in Michigan City. I was feverish around N., flushing; I felt the lightness I'd fought so hard for over the past years, and I wanted to share that with him. We drank chamomile tea together almost every night for the next few months. We joked about rats and Swiss Glacier Porn Stars and his hatred of parmesan. And I saw him panic. He said he felt like my heart was crowded; he wasn't wrong. I was trying to cycle through, rapidly, to inhabit the ever-opening space we were breathing into. He wanted to possess my time, as it were, in an improbable way. In the moment, I ignored his moments of quiet antagonism, how he found ways to senselessly critique our friends when we were in private. How that negativity seemed important to him.

    Still, we shared space. We went to Chicago together. We walked around a Halloween pop-up store, our bodies close as we looked at cheap plastic masks and wigs. We talked about going to San Juan in the spring. By the time winter came around, he had plans to go home to Japan. I, of course, had plans to go to Corona del Mar and Rome. We wrote each other letters, which we gave each other on the train when we said goodbye. I wanted to carry his voice.

    We sent each other photos of trees in Japan and California and Italy. We drank tea in sync despite the distance. Still, there was an ambiguous panic embedded in me; I had to circle through. I felt my body wheeling at the pace of a train, darting from South Bend to Chicago, and then so fast it looked static. I was either too fast, or too slow, and suddenly

I was imploding, panicking alone in Rome at five in the morning. I couldn't feel my legs, but they were trembling. I shook until sunrise, a painting of poppies overhead.

While I was in Rome, N. told me I didn't listen. Maybe he meant that I didn't hear him. Still, this was one of the worst things anyone could say to me. For weeks, he'd tell me one thing and then retract it. He'd accuse me and then comfort me, and then need me to comfort him. I questioned my every move, re-reading weeks of our correspondence. How could I listen, when I didn't know what he needed to communicate to me? I was destabilized, I was piercing static. My inability to stay open—if my listening wasn't that of receptivity to his being—became ambivalence.

It was a photo of complete blackness, I thought again and again to myself. I needed to breathe into myself, to break myself down. So, I turned to reading. I read a poem by Lyn Hejinian, from *Positions of the Sun*: "I am not a bra, nor a thriving coastal pine tree, nor a voyage; I am still ambivalent. [...] Pertinence, relevance ---- a constellating magnetic force of attraction ---- may intrude at any point and from any place, sourceless as time (though not otherwise resembling time)."

N. told me, of this writing, that I should dedicate a section to how I relate to myself. The suggestion was antithetical to my very being. In Hejinian's *Positions*, I saw relation both to and against external elements: a bra, a thriving coastal pine tree, a voyage. So, in the post-Rome winter, I got in touch with an old friend for advice. He told me that inviting external elements into one's clarity is a sacred practice, a relief. My clarity, my voice, makes space for relation. My writing is my body of relation. In this conversation, I was reminded that I'm empowered to choose who—and what—I relate to. That if I'm not met with empathy, I'm not safe.

As my ambivalence toward N. mutated, I began watching us from somewhere else, utterly removed from the wheel. Molasses-slow in my disassociation, I broke us apart. He just needed me to hold him in an empty room. I just needed to turn toward clarity, no matter the cost. Now, it's presence and loss. I hold it in my hands, cupped to nothing. There's more peace in that sound—a *hush*, the sound of still snow at dusk.

*

Is disassociation a semi-lucid and prolonged syncope? When I'm disassociated, I lose my body—all I can do is hear. Songs make impressions on me, bodiless, circling around—waiting for my being to catch up. The last night I spent with N., I heard "Terminal Paradise" in my mind as the snow fell outside. We held each other, but I was somewhere else, I wasn't me, I was snow snaking on the ground or pressed to the windowpane of my bedroom. *See my death become a trail, and the trail leads to a flower…every dreamed and waking hour.* I heard the song loop through my mind for hours. My body snaking snow, I imagined turning far from home, back to the Tyrrhenian Sea, the Tiber.

*

At the Capitoline Museums in Rome, I found myself alone in a room full of paintings of Mary. Upon seeing my favorite painting of her, I smiled to myself. I'd never seen it in person—I didn't even know which museum housed it. I found this one in a book called *Mary*, an archive of her being-in-art. I bought the book at the Art Institute of Chicago when I was sixteen. In this moment, I felt time folding over itself. This painting, tongue-pink over wood, depicted Mary with a bookshelf and an angel. What did she need to know?

As I moved further through the room, I saw a painting of Mary surrounded by her symbols: lily of the valley alongside harder-to-decipher images. Mary is suspended in a yellow orb, arms out as if to invoke properties of her symbols to sustain her vigilance. Her feet are cloaked by a crimson red dress, to further her flight—an illusion of hovering. Rather than the hovering of disassociation, of a syncope, Mary looks lucid. In a near-humorous way, I can imagine her asserting: *I'm here*.

*

In April, Will and I drove through Nashville listening to Josephine Foster's newest album, *Faithful Fairy Harmony*. When we lived together, we'd often drive around to listen to music. Something about listening to music in transit offered us a site of clarity. Whenever we'd finished recording and mixing a song of our own, we'd listen to its resonances and shortcomings from the space of Will's car. The longer we worked on a song from the comfort of our home, we lost perspective and sank into our subjectivities; we needed to hear it elsewhere. If the song didn't resonate from the car, it was doing something wrong. How the song interacted with the landscape—and with us in the landscape—would determine its success.

Will had reminded me that I'd been thinking about symbols long before the inception of this project. When we were seventeen, I wrote a song called "Syringe" about my abusive ex, a feverish Tom-Waits-esque piece at once playful and lamenting. In it, I sing: *I made my own religious signs*. Will and I recorded the songs on an old Wollensak tape machine in the basement of a dormitory at our high school, the static of the tape machine just as symbolic as the images I sang for. The static of the tape machine—my memory—churned, indecipherable, a haunt.

"Syringe," which I wrote during my ex's many disappearances and near-overdoses, during the vigilance he forced me to attend to by implicating me before his absence, was one among many attempts at healing. Even though the songs I wrote that fall were mostly about my ex, I named the album after myself: AM. I sang about magnolia trees, blue rosaries, a desert with crystal walls. The symbols were always for healing. Will saw that, affirmed that, and never asked me to explain myself—even as kids.

In the car, we listened to "The Virgin of the Snow." Josephine Foster opens the song by humming, until humming isn't enough, and her wordless singing takes on the qualities of vowels, prolongation: somewhere between an *ah* and an *oh*. The song, over six minutes long, ends just as it begins, in a hum—as if the song is a mirror, and only by looking into its reflection can a body come forth. Of all of Foster's music, I was floored by the gentle assuredness of "The Virgin"; she makes no effort to strain her voice, singing as if to lull a baby to sleep. She sings, certainly, of the virgin-as-gatekeeper. She sings about a silver sleigh, and the piano comes in to bolster the image. Cello floats just below her flying voice, doubling it, rendering her voice a force beyond body.

As we drove, Will and I wondered when the magnolia trees would bloom that spring. Nearly a year before, we had driven through Nashville wondering at the site of such blooms—saturated in their fragrance. I felt something fearlessly feminine in the strength and height and stature of the magnolia trees. Parallel to Shelby Park, near-blinding green out the windows, we marveled at the homes tucked behind the trees. We always imagined where we'd want to live—a bungalow, maybe. Some place small.

I felt time slow down as I watched the landscape—perhaps due to the spring-caused bloom, or the song's transcending movement, or both—and I said to Will quietly and with enough pause to emphasize how un-dramatic I wanted the statement to be, "I know it sounds crazy, but I feel the song un-rape me." It was a physically impossible utterance, but I felt held and empowered in my once-virginity as the song unfurled—as the cello and piano paralleled voice and offered flight. Will lifted a hand from his steering wheel, took it to hold my hand. He brought my hand to his lips and kissed it softly. I didn't need him to say anything. This was, I knew, the closest I'd get to healing.

*

 I got my favorite Virgin Mary at a junk store in downtown Missoula with a sign advertising "We Buy Anything" above the front door. She was translucent plastic and covered in dust. Despite all efforts at cleaning her, threads of dust pressed certainly into the creases of her form. I could see where her body had broken before—her head had snapped at the neck and was super-glued back on. I wondered who had repaired her, and what the circumstances of her beheading were. The supposed purity of her clear body, coupled by the dust and the cracks, presented a contradictory kind of virginity. I happily paid $10 and wrapped her in a T-shirt in my suitcase to bring home.

 Years later, when Carrot was a kitten, I heard a crash downstairs as I was changing clothes in my bedroom. When I descended the stairs, I saw that she had knocked a handful of picture frames off the top of a bookshelf, along with the Virgin. The noise of the crash must have been disturbing enough for Carrot—just a few months old, at that, just over the size of my outstretched palm—that she fled under the blue velvet couch before I could find her. When I crawled on the floor to look under the furniture, I eventually found Carrot out of reach behind the skirt of the couch, gnawing on the Virgin's head, severed once again.

*

    Resonating from the past, a week or years ago:
    Wild is the Wild – Xiu Xiu
    Janitor of Lunacy – Nico
    Stars – Nina Simone
    Riding for the Feeling – Bill Callahan
    Softly and Tenderly – Daniel Johnston

*

On Christmas Eve in Corona del Mar, I fainted in a church parking lot. I felt, in my veins, thousands of miniature wheels fluttering as they turned. I wasn't disassociated, but I forgot about my body. My mother and two brothers and I were driving to my grandparents' church. We'd meet my father and his parents in the parking lot, under the sea of olive trees and string lights, and walk inside together for an evening service.

My brothers and I were laughing about the repetitiveness of a L.A.-based hip hop radio station, and our mother laughed with us mostly out of confusion. While my mother was religious, my brothers and I had our refractions of spirituality and lack, sincerity and irreverence. Once the car was parked, I opened the door and got out and, as I slammed the door shut, caught my entire left thumb in the door.

Everyone was paces ahead of me now, but I was stuck in place. Ironically, it was the first moment I had to rest since Will had moved out. The wheel, my wheel, stuck. I struggled to cry out to my mother. When she turned around and saw my hand, I heard her scream pierce through the Christmas bells, the sounds of tires on cement, my grandmother's hushed voice.

I opened the car door. I saw the shape the door latch had carved into my thumb, close to the bone. I bled. By the time my brothers were by my side, I looked to my mom and said, "I'm going to faint soon." I collapsed onto my knees.

When I fell, I heard church bells, only bells. They were prolonged—by fainting, this literal syncope—and I felt myself bouncing around in space, slowly, in the metallic sounds of the bells, like wind. In the breath of space between a bell being struck. When I woke, the first thing I heard was Kurt calling my name. He was close to me, now, crouched to the ground to support me. I was covered in sweat. I was cold.

*

I only want to fill this space with bells, with olive trees.

I only want to fill this space with bells, with olive trees, with stone pines, with white pillows.

I only want to fill this space with two white moths, my body on pillows.

I only want to fill this space with German Shepherds on the seashore, my grandmother combing her hair, my grandfather tending to his garden. I only want to fill this space with bells, with olive trees, with stone pines, white pillows.

I only want to fill this space with—an inhalation—*For all—of god's angels—in heaven to sing.*

I only want to fill this space with pink flowers, with blood bloom, with blistered feet.

I only want to fill this space with white rock, clear rock, quartz rock, a clearing.

I only want to fill this space with white rock, clear rock, quartz rock, a clearing.

 I only want to fill this space with white rock, clear rock, quartz rock, a clearing.

I only want to fill this space with white rock, clear rock, quartz rock, a clearing.

I only want to fill this space with narrow hallways in Dublin as the slope of the wheel, waterfalls in Vermont as the slope of the wheel, the moment two distant hands touch, skin rough, veins pulsing.

I only want to fill this space with Tag, crouched beside a bonsai, ink pen in hand.

I only want to fill this space—Form of the Tree of Heaven.

I only want to fill this space with well water, lake water, the sound of a voice reverberating on its waves, into its structure.

*

    In his foreword to *Purgatorio*, W. S. Merwin notes that the epic ends with "Beatrice, at a moment of unfathomable loss and exposure, [calling] the poem's narrator and protagonist by name, 'Dante', and the […] sound of his name at that moment is not at all reassuring. Would it ever be? And who would it reassure?" Naming at this site of loss and exposure… in a banal way, I see my brother's voice while I was unconscious, and then waking me, as enacting this. Naming at this site of loss and exposure…I see my older brother supporting my mother. I see my father driving me to the emergency room, Kurt by my side. I see my grandparents sitting quietly in their sanctuary, candlelight around their faces.

    Alice Notley writes that "a voice itself," "a woman's voice with access to the mystery of the dream," is Epic. This voice, according to Notley, need be "circuitous," a force of "winding." Perhaps, after Merwin, there is no reassurance in being named. The act of naming necessitates a vigilance to the speaker and the receiver. Kurt called for me, and I came back from my dream of bells.

*

I need you to listen with me.

> [*Let It Be Me*. Nina Simone.
> "Stars"; four minutes, thirty-three seconds.]

When Will and I first reconnected, he sent me a video of Nina Simone performing "Stars." I watched it, hypnotized—in bed, in the dark. She sings: "if you don't mind being patient with my fumbling around, I'll come up singing for you." In the same way John Jacob Niles leans into the prolongation of "you" and "I" in "I Wonder as I Wander," Simone makes space for being-with. For a moment, I felt the ceaseless turning of my past decade suspended by her voice—coaxed to momentary stillness. This suspension is in every pause between her articulations of the piano, its slow and circuitous rhythm. Her articulations of the piano mimic that of bells—with steady rhythm, minimal chords, and pause rich enough for other resonances. Here, piano makes way for voice.

And, in the video, as she performed live at Montreux Jazz Festival in 1971, she commands her audience to sit down before continuing. The audience laughs, but she repeats: *sit down, sit down*. The request is grave. As her eyes look intently past the camera and into the audience, it doesn't look like she's singing for anyone in her midst. In her eyes, accented by a clay-colored glitter eyeshadow, I see sincere inwardness while exhibiting an ambivalence toward her audience. She doesn't need to perform her vigilance: *I'm trying to tell my story*, she sings. But I don't think this audience is who she's intending to tell it to. She tells it for herself, trusting its weight.

I can't remember it anyway, she continues, falling into a larger space for vocal pause. This pause, a suspension, is one I see my body turning to now. This pause, a suspension, carries me through olive trees, stone pines, metal stars pressed into the cobblestone streets of Trastevere. *Purgatorio* ends with stars, too. *Purgatorio* ends with stars—and, in its celestial ending, opens itself for Nina Simone. Dante couldn't know.

The piano keeps her going until it swells. The piano swells just as she sings of other musicians: Janis Joplin, Billie Holiday. Then she returns to the 'we'. *We always have a story*. I recall a video of the pianist Glenn Gould entering a trance as he plays Bach's Partita #2 at home in his bathrobe. He doubles his piano performance with his voice. Until, midway through, he stands from the piano, turns around, walks to the window, looks out to the birds in his yard. He hums the song in perfect tempo from the moment his fingers leave the keys to the moment he returns. He turns around after some time, returns to the piano, and keeps playing as if no compulsive interruption occurred.

I see myself—I see my memory—in this space of turning, re-turning. I wonder where Gould goes when he rises from the piano. I wonder where Simone goes when she tilts her head back, closes her eyes, inhales before continuing to sing.

That night of reconnection, I watched the video of her performance a dozen times, my phone close to my face. I drifted with Nina Simone's face next to mine until my phone went dark, until I couldn't hold my eyes open, until I woke hours later to the sun shining outside and my cat tapping my pillow-turned cheek with her paw. Nina Simone's voice—*perhaps they have a soul they aren't afraid to bear*. This fearlessness doesn't pull her out of the song. Instead, she repeats herself. She stutters, she stumbles, it's what she's supposed to go out with.

She repeats herself. She repeats herself. Voice becoming symbol.

Endnotes

*   Gaston Bachelard, *The Poetics of Space*

†   Laurie Anderson, the Watermill Center, July 2017

‡   Walter Benjamin, "Sketched in Mobile Dust"

§   Lyrics from "Ribbon Bow" by Karen Dalton and "Song to the Siren" by Tim Buckley

¶   From Richard Cullen Rath's "No Corner for the Devil to Hide": "Taken together, the chancel and its parts constituted a sort of reverberant sound amplifier. Because the signal was already reverberating before it left the chancel and because a chancel is much larger than a guitar, the sound emitted from it at any moment was a compendium of echoes, the sources of which overlapped in time much more so than those coming from a lute. [...] Sounds bounced around echo upon echo upon echo rather than reaching the listener's ears all at once. This created a powerfully moving effect, one that amplified the voice and enriched the tone, but at the cost of clarity. Acoustician Hope Bagenal somewhat derisively describes the emphasis on reverberant sound found in Catholic churches as the 'acoustics of the cave', comparing it with the acoustics of the open air exemplified by Greek amphitheaters and, implicitly, Protestantism."

**   "Is 'X' the breath of the it? the cold radiating respiration of it? Is "X" a word? The word only refers to a thing and is always unreachable by me."

Selected Sources

Alighieri, Dante. *Purgatorio: A New Verse Translation*. Translated by W. S. Merwin, Knopf, 2000.

Chion, Michel. *Sound: An Acoulogical Treatise*. Duke University Press, 2016.

Clément, Catherine. *Syncope: The Philosophy of Rapture*. Translated by Deirdre M. Mahoney and Sally O'Driscoll, University of Minnesota Press, 1994.

Deleuze, Gilles. *Difference and Repetition*. Translated by Paul Patton, Columbia University Press, 1995.

Farley, Helen. *A Cultural History of Tarot: From Entertainment to Esotericism*. Bloomsbury Academic, 2019.

Hejinian, Lyn. *Positions of the Sun*. Belladonna*, 2018.

Lispector, Clarice. *Água Viva*. Translated by Stefan Tobler, New Directions Books, 2012.

Notley, Alice. *Coming After: Essays on Poetry*. University of Michigan Press, 2005.

Notley, Alice. *The Descent of Alette*. Penguin Poets, 1996.

Reines, Ariana. "BARAKA." *Fence*, vol. 14, nos. 1 + 2, 2011.

Serafini, Luigi. *Codex Seraphinianus*. Rizzoli, 2013.

Teare, Brian. "The Best Job on Earth: On the Poetry of C. D. Wright." *Poetry Foundation*, 2017.

Weil, Simone. *Gravity and Grace*. Translated by Emma Crawford and Mario Von der Ruhr, Routledge Classics, 2002.

Acknowledgments

Thank you, with inarticulable gravity, to Mary Steege and Suzi Naiburg. Thank you to Ben Johnston-Krase and Julie Avis Rogers. Thank you to Maria Koundoura and Pablo Muchnik. Thank you to Trish Hartland, Lavinia Xu and Christina Leo. Thank you to the MFA in Creative Writing Program at the University of Notre Dame, particularly Joyelle McSweeney, Romana Huk and Steve Tomasula. Thank you to Johannes Göransson and Sabrina Orah Mark for the 2019 Sparks Prize, which allowed me to finish this book. Thank you to my longtime teachers and friends, Nick Demske and Chris Dombrowski. Thank you to Kelly Conger, Amandla Colón, Anne Tsaloff, Saoli Nash and Cinthya Oyervides. Thank you to my family, forever, whose love and humor fills me. Thank you to Will, forever, for the humility and honesty we are continually learning to live by. Thank you for listening with me.

AM RINGWALT is a writer and musician. Her creative and critical writing appears in *Jacket2*, *Black Warrior Review*, *Washington Square Review* and *Bennington Review*. *Waiting Song* is her most recent record.

www.ingramcontent.com/pod-product-compliance
Lightning Source LLC
Chambersburg PA
CBHW051806100526
44592CB00016B/2578